THE SOCIAL MEDIA MBA

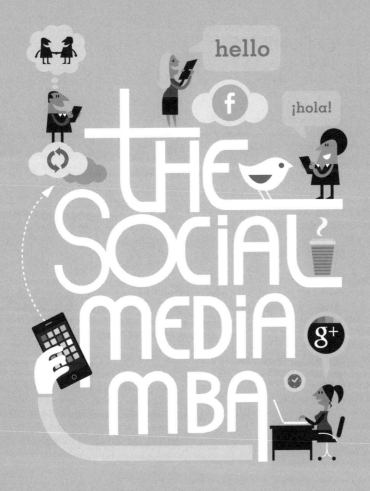

THE SOCIAL MEDIA MBA

Your Competitive Edge in Social Media Strategy Development & Delivery

Christer Holloman

Co-authors: Eb Adeyeri, Johan Bergelin, Ged Carroll, Jed Hallam, Tim Hoang, Neville Hobson, David Marrinan-Hayes, Michael Netzley, Zaheer Nooruddin, Euan Semple, Max Tatton-Brown, Boris Veldhuijzen van Zanten, Jeremy Woolf, Alex Yenni and Simon Young.

A John Wiley & Sons, Ltd., Publication

Registered office
John Wiley & Sons Ltd, The Atrium, Southern Gate, Chichester, West Sussex, PO19 8SQ, United Kingdom

For details of our global editorial offices, for customer services and for information about how to apply for permission to reuse the copyright material in this book please see our website at http://www.wiley.com/go/permissions

Wiley publishes in a variety of print and electronic formats and by print-on-demand. Some material included with standard print versions of this book may not be included in e-books or in print-on-demand. If this book refers to media such as a CD or DVD that is not included in the version you purchased, you may download this material at http://booksupport.wiley.com. For more information about Wiley products, visit www.wiley.com.

Designations used by companies to distinguish their products are often claimed as trademarks. All brand names and product names used in this book are trade names, service marks, trademarks or registered trademarks of their respective owners. The publisher is not associated with any product or vendor mentioned in this book. This publication is designed to provide accurate and authoritative information in regard to the subject matter covered. It is sold on the understanding that the publisher is not engaged in rendering professional services. If professional advice or other expert assistance is required, the services of a competent professional should be sought.

Library of Congress Cataloging-in-Publication Data

Holloman, Christer.
The social media MBA : your competitive edge in social media strategy development and delivery / Christer Holloman ; co-authors, Eb Adeyeri . . . [et al.].
    p. cm.
Includes bibliographical references and index.
ISBN 978-1-119-96323-3
   1. Information technology–Management.   2. Social media.   3. Customer relations.   4. Internet marketing.   5. Branding (Marketing)   I. Adeyeri, Eb.   II. Title.
HD30.2.H645 2012
658.8'72–dc23

                                                        2011044310

A catalogue record for this book is available from the British Library.

ISBN 978-1-119-96323-3 (hardback) ISBN 978-1-119-96722-4 (ebk)
ISBN 978-1-119-96723-1 (ebk)   ISBN 978-1-119-96724-8 (ebk)

Typeset in 10/14.5 pt FF Scala by Toppan Best-set Premedia Limited, Hong Kong
Printed in Great Britain by TJ International Ltd, Padstow, Cornwall, UK

CONTENTS

PREFACE

Resources allocated, strategies drafted, tweets posted but the lord's work is never done

This book is the first of its kind in the third and final wave of social media literature. It is targeting professionals like you, who work for organizations that already use social media and have been doing so for a while.

I was in your shoes about 18 months ago. I worked as a consultant for a subsidiary of a British media conglomerate when they asked me to review their social media strategy. In my case, it turned out that this so called strategy was pretty undefined. Their execution mainly focused on blogging and the method of measuring the return was rudimentary to say the least. When it became clear that this company was barely scratching the surface of what they could achieve with social media I had a very strong intuitive feeling in my stomach that this was an amazing opportunity for me to really make a difference.

Whatever your continent, industry, company size, current degree of social media adoption or job title, the purpose of this book is to inspire you to see your situation as I saw mine. It will give you the tools to make a difference to your organization's social media strategy development and delivery going forward. In addition it will also give you further intellectual support and the confidence to discuss social media on a higher level with peers, inspire colleagues or negotiate and create support for additional investments from your leadership team.

Why I created this book

When I was about to embark on the social media strategy review journey explained above, I looked high and low for literature and advice that could help me. I quickly established that until now there seem to have been two waves of social media books:

- First were the theoretical books of almost social anthropological nature, talking about the potential of Web 2.0, user generated content as the new democracy, the power of online communities and so on. Everything felt like yesterday's news, was too theoretical to actually be useful and didn't offer any hands on advice for businesses.
- The second wave came when companies realized that everyone was "doing" social media and they wanted to "get on it". These books are like ABC guides for kids, how to get more followers on Twitter, how to write a good blog post and so on. Helpful about two years ago yes, but this kind of advice is far too elementary for people like us.

There were also a couple of other things that annoyed me about all the materials I came across: mainly that they were written by some self acclaimed "expert". Why should anyone trust what one person says about anything? Finally, most social media books available today are written by US authors with a US perspective. How does this translate to the global reality of aspiring businesses? No one uses Twitter in China!

I figured it was time for a new generation of books on this topic.

How I created it

I set out to make the book I couldn't find, that addressed all the issues I had come across in my own market research, pitched at a social media maturity level relevant for my organization today.

The first decision I made was not to write this book alone, I wanted the best people to share their experiences. The second decision was that I would not only work with people from a particular region, but across the globe.

Thirdly I wanted a mix of contributors from the corporate side as well as the agency world, representing companies and clients ranging from manufacturing to services, from B2C to B2B, from high end to high street.

Through my role as technology trend commentator for *Sky News* and chairman of First Tuesday UK I have had the opportunity to get to know Eb Adeyeri over the years in his capacity as the Digital Director at Lewis PR. I've always admired his refreshing no nonsense business approach to social media. I ran my idea past him and asked if he wanted to be a part of it: he said yes straight away. When I asked him whom he follows and turns to for social media inspiration, he gave me some names that I added to my own list. I continued to invite people from the list and those that said yes I asked the same question to. So it went on until I had 15 peer reviewed and approved co-authors from four continents and case studies from eight global and local brands, each prepared by their respective social media leader.

Given my brief, as outlined earlier, and with you as our intended target audience we collaboratively brainstormed chapter ideas. From that the structure was developed and everyone set to work. The title was born later, when it became obvious that we had created nothing short of a specialized MBA. Just like a traditional MBA you will be blasted by stimulating ideas from a range of lecturers to set you up for impressing at work, not to mention access to a global alumni network of industry peers.

For more information about the co-authors and their contact details, should you like to connect with them directly, please see the Biography section at the end of the book.

Structure

There are five sections to this book, but feel free to jump between the chapters as the headlines capture your attention. Each chapter starts with a brief summary of what to expect, so you quickly understand how it could be relevant for you.

While working on this project the co-authors have seen each other's headlines and top level outlines but not the actual chapters. This means that there will be instances of natural cross over and repetition regarding some the most important concepts. Take that as a hint for what may come on the exam later. Only joking, there is no exam. Think of repetition as a second chance to internalize the information.

In the same way that different lecturers addressing a class each have their own personality, so will the style of each chapter slightly vary in this book.

We start with the Foundation. Although this book is targeting representatives of organizations that have been using social media for more than a year, think of this as a refresher and a chance for everyone else to get on the same page, if you pardon the pun.

The main sections address Strategy Development & Delivery. We believe that the social media strategy and delivery plan, whether a stand-alone document or part of your overall communication plan, must be a living document. The best companies are always prepared to try new ideas and revise their plans accordingly.

The fourth section is Case Studies. We have asked those responsible for the social media strategy at a diverse group of companies to share highlights from recent success stories, budgets, results, their best advice and more. As different companies define sensitive information differently the amount of detail disclosed varies somewhat in each case study.

The final section, The Future, will get you thinking about the next steps beyond this book and maybe even beyond social media as we know it today.

With all that said, I think we are set to invite our first lecturer so that classes may commence. Sharpen your pens!

P.S. Are you a member of The Social Media MBA Alumni network yet?

As I alluded earlier, there is an alumni network of fellow readers, people around the world that work professionally with social media. This is a great place to exchange ideas, ask questions or perhaps look around for new job openings or recruit a member to your team. Join by visiting http://www.socialmedia-mba.com or search for "The Social Media MBA Alumni" on LinkedIn.

Christer Holloman
Zürich, January 2012

Part I

Foundation

Chapter 1

Neville Hobson

In short

- Why social media isn't about different websites, but people.
- How to recognize need for change.
- What to listen out for before speaking.

Overview

In this chapter London-based Neville Hobson – early adopter, opinion-leader and influencer in social media communication for business – will discuss how introducing social media into an organization means change. Change in the way everyone understands how the organization works. Social media is disruptive, challenging established orders, hierarchies and cultures. You can't stop disruption, but you can harness it and make its introduction a less painful process than it may seem. You need to find a new way of looking at your organization and how you can get things done.

With all the talk you hear about Facebook, Twitter, YouTube, LinkedIn, Google+ and other social places online – you name it, people talk about it when they mention social media – it wouldn't be too much of a surprise to think that social media is all about Facebook, Twitter and the like.

> Social media isn't about the tools and the channels – the software or the technology.

Yet it's not. Social media isn't about the tools and the channels – the software or the technology. It's all about *what people do with the technology*, the software, the tools and the channels: sharing pictures and video, writing product reviews, collecting content, connecting with old friends, sharing with new friends, collaborating in the workplace.

Social media is a collective term that describes the means of communicating and engaging with people. It's something many people see as evolutionary, if not revolutionary, in helping people connect with each other in ways that are genuine, authentic and natural.

However you see it, social media usage is increasing rapidly and dramatically in all levels of society and in more countries around the world. And businesses of all shapes and sizes are embracing it.

Introducing social media into an organization usually means change: change in the way everyone understands how the organization works. It often means change in the ways people relate to and connect with others, inside and outside the organization. And change in their roles and responsibilities where what had seemed clear to everyone perhaps isn't any more.

For the organization, social media can be hugely disruptive, challenging established orders, hierarchies and cultures. You can't stop disruption, but you can embrace it and make the introduction of a new way of doing things a less painful process than it may initially seem.

> The benefits of taking a calculated risk to embrace social media as a legitimate business tool are clear and compelling to many companies who have taken the first steps.

The benefits of taking a calculated risk to embrace social media as a legitimate business tool are clear and compelling to many companies who have taken the first steps. For them, social media today is an integral element in their marketing, public relations and overall approach to building business relationships.

The key word is *calculated*. The stakes are high: everything you do should be considered against objectives you can measure. You need to see a new way of looking at your organization and the people it comprises, and create the environment that lets them get things done effectively and with confidence.

Following are five tips to point the way.

1. Recognize change

The web is rapidly evolving and is having a big impact on millions of people's behaviours in countries around the world. Little more than a decade ago, all you could really do was read static content on websites. Today, you can *create* rich and interactive content on websites from anywhere in the world where there's a network connection, on almost any kind of device, wired or wireless. Anyone can do this, not just the big companies of the past decade.

This society-level change means we're seeing disruption to traditional business models and new ideas springing up on how people want to communicate and connect using social media – the new tools of the web – whether for personal interests or to get things done at work.

From giving a concise opinion on Twitter, checking in on Foursquare, to saying "Like" on Facebook, there is a dramatic shift in people's behaviours, which manifests itself in the changes in how we communicate online, with whom, where we do it and when.

Another way of looking at it is to consider changes in our social structures in which easier technology puts power in the hands of individuals and communities instead of only organizations and institutions.

Why should we care? Because social media is changing how marketing and communication works and how people want to connect with brands. It presents an organization with an affordable way to get measurable results quickly when it's employed

> Why should we care? Because social media is changing how marketing and communication works and how people want to connect with brands.

effectively. It's rapidly growing, and customers turn to their peers for answers increasingly using social networks and other online tools and channels – precisely the places where today's organization needs to be present, too, in the right way.

It's an unmistakable trend. You only need to look around you to see it happening right in front of your eyes.

2. Make a deal with your employees to eliminate FUD

What often holds organizations back from introducing any aspect of social media – whether it's a single public blog, uploading video to YouTube or creating a brand page on Facebook or Google+ – are fear, uncertainty and doubt:

- **Fear** of perceived security risks in allowing employees access to social media tools and channels: "What if someone stole our secrets or released them without permission, or brought a virus into our network?"
- **Uncertainty** over the effects of losing control: "Isn't there a huge risk that employees will say something they shouldn't if we don't monitor what they're allowed to do?"
- **Doubt** over productivity: "Surely it increases the chances for employees to waste time?"

While you can learn from examples of how other organizations have addressed such concerns – just Google the phrase "concerns about social media" – you can also cut to the chase and begin your calculated risk assessment by starting with creating a climate of trust with your employees.

Such a contemporary approach in the workplace sees employer and employee in a partnership where, through the establishment of trust and mutual respect over time, each partner recognizes the critical stake the other has in the organization's success and how enabling employees, with effective tools, to engage with others online can measurably benefit the organization and support its business goals.

A key component of the climate of trust is helping everyone understand what the rules of engagement are – in essence, what's permitted and what's not when employees reach out to others via social channels – as well as an ongoing education framework where employees have access to formal and informal learning opportunities to help them gain knowledge of and confidence in the tools and channels available to them.

Developing policies and guidelines are key building blocks in your engagement planning, and demonstrate your willingness as the employer to foster a trust climate, especially when development is carried out jointly rather than only via the traditional employer-to-employee cascade system.

None of these essential foundational activities as elements in your overall risk assessment will actually eliminate the perceived risks associated with letting go of control. What they can do is eliminate the FUD.

3. Be where your customers are

Engaging with customers on their terms, not yours, is a prerequisite for building genuine and sustainable online relationships. The days are long gone when a primary marketing goal was to make your website "sticky", where visitors came to your site and didn't leave. Nowadays, the goal is to offer your visitors content they will value – even if that content is at places other than yours.

> What consumers want are honesty, transparency and authenticity.

What consumers want are honesty, transparency and authenticity. For companies, this means having a genuine and open personality, one that reflects today's new consumer values. Therefore, the people in the company must be visible and engaged with people outside the company, talking with customers in their own genuine and individual voices.

Research shows that customers typically like to do three things online:

1. **Share ideas** – "Let's improve the next product or service together."
2. **Share product knowledge** – "Here is what I know . . . I hope it helps you."
3. **Help peers with problems** – "I had the same problem, here is what I did."

Many individuals in companies recognize this and they join the conversation as well, becoming part of their customers' peer group, and gaining better understanding of what their customers want.

Nowhere is this more true than with social networking sites – increasingly places of choice for consumers and groups to publicly share opinions, recommendations and criticism of brands and products.

In most countries today, Facebook is either the most popular or second or third most popular website. The social network has reached such widespread popularity that it can these days only really be compared to Google, the only other company that can claim a similar reach. Yet while more than 800 million people globally are regular Facebook users (the figure in September 2011), don't ignore domestic social networks in the countries that interest you with memberships still in the millions. Which service you use to connect with customers and others doesn't only depend on the numbers – you need to be where your customers are, whether that's Facebook or somewhere else.

A clear consumer trend is wide rejection of the concept of the corporate voice, where the organization spoke and it was never clear who was speaking. The companies who genuinely promote brand plus individual will enjoy the most influence: wherever the customer prefers to be.

4. Listen

Getting started with social media doesn't mean you have to create a Facebook page for your business or open a Twitter account. On the contrary – your first step isn't talking, it's listening.

In fact, there are three simple steps you can easily follow that will not only give you valuable insight into how others see you and what they say about you online but will also give you insight and confidence on what your next steps should be.

1. When you listen carefully, you'll know your customer's world online *with precision*. No more guesswork.
2. That learning will help you focus on actionable insights – what exactly can inform your planning.

3. That will help you identify who drives share of conversation. In other words, who you should pay attention to – with whom you might engage.

You can take your first step today. Ask yourself what you are going to listen *for*. You need to be clear in your focus.

- Are you listening (monitoring social media, in other words) for reputation management or customer service reasons?
- Do you want to gather business intelligence and get feedback on your brand?
- Are you looking to find conversations you can join so your organization can get exposure in front of new audiences?
- Do you want to keep an eye on your competition?
- Are you planning prudently in the eventuality of a crisis?

This is what two organizations have most definitely recognized, according to AdAge.com, which showcases the stellar examples of Kodak and Dell, both of which have Chief Listening Officers.

The advent of social media has brought the topic of listening to the forefront of organizations' communication planning, internally and externally. During the past decade, especially in the past couple of years, we've seen social media become a significant element in the strategic approach to communication in many organizations. Some best practices are emerging, too.

We've also seen the emergence of new roles to bring individuals with wisdom and insight to the communication mix where everyone has an opinion and ideas that often require significant structure for them to be viable in an organization setting.

Enter the Chief Social Media Officer, a job title that sprang up in the US a year or so ago. The case for a CSMO role was well argued by Jennifer Leggio. So I wonder how a Chief Listening Officer will do.

In my view, such a role implied by the title is surely and exactly what organizations need today, especially large organizations. It's not enough just to listen to conversations, analyze what's going on and interpret the metrics: you need to know exactly, *with precision*, what the huge amount of interpreted data means to your organization specifically and what the people in their different roles can and must do as a result of the knowledge and insights you've gleaned from that listening, from that interpretation of the data.

Above all, you must know who in your organization needs what information, and be able to get that information to those people, on demand, when they need it.

Such a role isn't necessarily one for someone with a communication background. That's the case for Chief Listener at Dell Susan Beebe, who told AdAge that her job is "complex."

> "There is a data-analysis research role to this job, and I have a very technical background," Ms. Beebe said. Dell has thousands of new mentions per day and the CLO's job is one of "broad listening" – as Dell has such a deep penetration globally in so many different markets.
>
> Unlike many social-media jobs, this position is very inward-facing. She's listening to Dell customers and consumers and giving all the intel to her Dell colleagues internally.
>
> "Our chief listener is critical to making sure the right people in the organization are aware of what the conversations on the web are saying about us, so that relevant people in the business can connect with customers," said Richard Binhammer, communications executive at Dell. Mr. Binhammer points out that "Dell has been listening for four years and created a position called 'Listening Czar' two years ago. We are a leader in the listening space."

Another leader is Kodak, whose Chief Listening Officer Beth LaPierre says that data mining and figuring out who needs the information is her "big task."

> "We get about 300,000 new mentions of Kodak every month and we don't censor the comments or videos people create about our company"[...] "I've spent the past five months defining how we handle those data via technology and tools."
>
> [...] "What kind of information does our marketing team need vs. our product team?" Ms. LaPierre said. "How do we classify the data? What is the process for handling 'ABC' information vs. 'XYZ' information?" For example, she sends commentary about features and product requests to a product development team and so forth.

These are great insights, ones to give careful attention to as you consider what you need to do in your organization as part of your engagement planning and attempt to understand the real value of listening as a strategic business tool.

5. Permit not prohibit

If there's one critical element in an organization's approach to empowering and enabling employees to go out there on the public web and engage with other people, it's helping them via education and training to know and understand how to conduct themselves in accordance with the organization's wishes. It's a key part of the risk assessment you would conduct when deciding on your approach to digital communication in general and social media in particular.

It's adding substance to the simple phrase "This is how we do things around here."

If you don't have ground rules established and communicated to employees, and their agreement to follow them secured, then you don't have much basis for creating the right environment or framework for your employees to do their jobs effectively, never mind the more fundamental aspects of trust in the workplace. Indeed, any climate of confidence or trust is much diminished in such circumstances.

Let's consider for a moment the picture where the employer swings entirely the other way and restricts or outright prohibits access to the social web in the workplace.

A survey published in 2010 by Cisco Systems, conducted among medium-to-large enterprises in ten countries, describes the scene very clearly indeed for what typically happens in organizations that do have access restrictions imposed in the workplace and where employees then take matters into their own hands:

> Half admit to accessing prohibited applications once a week, and more
> than a quarter admit to changing the settings on their devices to gain
> access in order to "get the job done."

- Slightly more than half (52 percent) of organizations prohibit the use of social media applications or similar collaboration tools at work.
- Half (50 percent) of the end users admit to ignoring company policy prohibiting use of social media tools at least once a week, and 27 percent admit to changing the settings on corporate devices to get access to prohibited applications.

The easiest ways for employees to circumvent workplace restrictions are outside the workplace, not on the organization network (computer at home, for instance, or using one in an internet cafe) or using one's mobile device, whether work-provided or personal (and it's increasingly common to see employees in the workplace with their own iPhone or other smartphone or tablet to complement the corporate BlackBerry).

Yet surely the better solution is communication and engagement. Examine all the choices in front of you as an organization: weigh up the pros and cons of enabling employee access to social networks and other places out there on the web or letting them use apps to "get things done." Involve employees in creating guidelines (IBM set the benchmark for that way back in 2005) so that everyone is clear on what is allowed and what isn't.

> The real challenge for decision makers in the organization is grappling with their fear of the unknown

It isn't hard to manage social media. The real challenge for decision makers in the organization is grappling with their fear of the unknown, their fear of giving up control over information, and being clear about everyone's expectations. Companies who use social media for business advantage and have developed effective training and education programmes and publish their guidelines – whether they call them policies, guidelines, tips or whatever best suits the way they do things – will find their employees more likely to advocate their products and services and become their own brand ambassadors. People want to work there because there is mutual trust demonstrated.

Make *informed* decisions. Isn't it that simple?

Roundup

Want more? See what has been said about this chapter or get involved and discuss it with the author and other readers on our LinkedIn group, find it by visiting http://www.socialmedia-mba.com or search for "The Social Media MBA Alumni".

This introduction is for those that haven't yet embarked on a strategy-based social media journey, as this is a prerequisite to enjoying the full benefit of the rest of the book.

A key point to remember from this chapter is that social media isn't a passing trend, it's simply a new method to allow us humans to do what we have always been doing; interacting and sharing information with each other. The difference now is just that it happens faster than before, which is putting pressure on you to become the expert over night, develop an appropriate action plan and deliver results.

Bridging the gap between the way we used to work and a new norm that incorporates social media should be your end goal. In the next chapter Jeremy Woolf provides you with the first set of tools to help you do so successfully.

References

Adage.com, "'Chief Listeners' Use Technology to Track, Sort Company Mentions", August 30, 2010 http://adage.com/article/digital/marketing-chief-listeners-track-brand-mentions/145618/.

Cisco press release, "Employees Poised to Collaborate More as Enterprises Plan to Invest in Collaboration Technology During 2010", March 23, 2010. http://newsroom.cisco.com/dlls/2010/prod_032310.html.

IBM, "IBM Social Computing Guidelines: Blogs, wikis, social networks, virtual worlds and social media" http://www.ibm.com/blogs/zz/en/guidelines.html.

ZDNet, "Is it time for a Chief Social Media Officer?", April 16, 2009 http://www.zdnet.com/blog/feeds/is-it-time-for-a-chief-social-media-officer/1010.

Chapter 2

Why no company can avoid social media and those that do will fail

Jeremy Woolf

In short

- How social media has changed society and how companies must change with it.
- The evolution from business to social business.
- Who should run your social media (not the office intern!).

Overview

There's a yawning chasm between social media perception and reality.

In this chapter Jeremy Woolf, Senior Vice President and Global Social Media and Digital Lead at Text 100 (http://www.text100.com/) based in Hong Kong, will help you understand that a) you haven't missed the boat, and b) that those furtive first steps may have been a waste of time but that's ok as long as you know where you're going (and can correct your course!).

This last point is critical – unless you understand the destination and focus on incremental change, you'll struggle.

Using international real-world examples, practical steps you can take to ensure you're using social media channels appropriately and with purpose are discussed.

It has been 20 years since Geoffrey A. Moore published his seminal marketing tome, *Crossing the Chasm*. Moore's core tenet was that there is a significant gap in technology buying – between the enthusiastic "early adopters" and other customer segments led by the pragmatic "early majority". He believed marketers should create programmes for one group of customers at a time, and then use each group to help market to the next group.

Though first published in 1991, *Crossing the Chasm* is still shaping marketing decisions today. But, in many other ways, 1991 was a long time ago. Bryan Adams topped the billboard charts with his *Robin Hood* love song, *(Everything I Do) I Do It For You*. Rosanne Barr's *Rosanne* show led the television ratings while in the Middle East, Operation Desert Storm pushed Iraq's forces out of Kuwait. It was also the year a new thing called the World Wide Web became publicly available on the internet (whose global population was in the low millions). Fast forward 20 years: the internet now is home to more than two billion people. More than 70 per cent of the world's internet population visits social networking sites. At the time of writing, Facebook's (www .facebook.com) active user population is more than 750 million (and counting). And each minute another 35 hours of video is uploaded to YouTube (www.youtube.com).

The catalyst for this is what we've come to call "Web 2.0" technology. Web 2.0 is a term made popular by technology guru Tim O'Reilly in 2003. O'Reilly put forward the idea of the web as a "platform"; where software applications were built upon the web as opposed to the PC desktop. This migration has enabled a new age, according to O'Reilly, in which "customers are building your business for you" (O'Reilly and Battelle, 2004). These were prophetic words that businesses nine years later are only just starting to hear.

And while organizations start to listen, the dramatic internet uptake driven by O'Reilly's Web 2.0 tools has created a whole new type of chasm – one with repercussions that go far beyond simple technology adoption. This new chasm is shaped by social media – and represents the gap between consumer need and the businesses scrambling rapidly to meet their requirements.

Clearly, social media channels are no longer the playthings of the tech elite or "pyjama-wearing" bloggers raging at the moon from the comfort of their parents' basements. Social media has been credited with helping elect Barack Obama to the White House – and raising more than USD500 million in donations. Twitter (www.twitter.com) has brought us real time coverage of major events such as the May 2011 raid on Osama bin Laden's compound. And from the blogging world, a Korean blogger known as "Mephisto" was prosecuted for posts that prompted the Korean Government to invest billions to stabilize its currency.

Add to this the fact that the fastest growing demographics on Facebook and other social networking sites are the over 50s, and clearly the game is changing. With this come changes to the nature of relationships. Take China, for example, where youth have more online friends than offline. Increasingly digital destinations such as Twitter, Facebook, LinkedIn and YouTube are having a profound effect on relationships, forcing businesses to change the way they work with their key audiences.

But why? What's catalyzed the shift from geek to chic? From my perspective, the answer is one that has much more to do with anthropology than technology. Web 2.0 technologies have enabled three very old and fundamental human desires; namely to share, to collaborate and to create. Tens of thousands of years ago, our Neanderthal forebears first gathered to share the spoils of the hunt, sharpen their tools and paint bison on the walls of their caves. Today, little has changed other than that new technologies have made it easier for people to realize these three core desires.

Unless the global internet kill switch is enabled, this isn't going away. Those end-is-nigh fatalists who believe social media is a fad are destined to be disappointed and our smartest business leaders have seen the writing on the digital "wall". The logic is sound and the evidence is mounting. McKinsey's December 2010 The Rise of the Networked Enterprise study (Bughin and Chui, 2010) of thousands of executives determined that technology-enabled collaboration with external stakeholders helps organizations gain market share from the competition. It also concluded that web technologies raise productivity and help create more valuable products and services resulting in higher profits.

So while many companies cry "resource limitations" and "lack of ROI", the world is changing around them. Facebook CEO Mark Zuckerberg succinctly summed up the required changes during his company's sFund event in October 2010. He said:

> There's going to be an opportunity over the next five years or so to pick any industry and rethink it in a social way . . . we think that every industry is going to be fundamentally re-thought and designed around people. (Shiels, 2010)

Now admittedly, Mr Zuckerberg – as the creator of the world's largest social network – has a vested interest in companies re-designing themselves around people. But it is hard to fault his logic. The people have spoken and they want change. And, perhaps what's most critical is that they want change across the board. While many marketers have rather crassly embraced social media as a way of simply amplifying their output, the potential value goes well beyond clicks on a press release or amassing a follower count in the hundreds of thousands.

People are inherently social creatures and increasingly demand social interaction from the companies they buy from, work for, partner with and so on. For example, the days of customer support being available between 9am and 6pm on weekdays are numbered. Customers expect a response and if they don't get one, they'll tweet or blog about it. If you want the latest shoes, you're purchasing in real time based on the aggregated votes of a peer community via Zappos Mappos (http://www.zappos.com/). If you're meeting with prospective employers, you're likely to spend time on Glassdoor.com (http://www.glassdoor.com) checking out what employees have said about their companies on the corporate websites.

The tone is now being set for businesses by their customers, staff and business partners – and companies must adapt. More critically, they must participate.

This is certainly easier said than done as participation in online communities appears in very few job descriptions. Companies are increasingly encouraging employees to participate in social media channels – but what does this mean for traditional media relations? In this new age of engagement, has the old-school corporate spokesperson gone the way of the dodo? Is it a case of Darwinian survival of the fittest, where only those who can traverse the often murky social media landscape will survive? And for those that are walking the talk, can they separate their personal and public brands? Or are the two entwined in some kind of Anakin Skywalker/Darth Vader-esque embrace?

Many questions, to which there are many answers. Historically, the corporate message has been sculpted in boardrooms, drilled into sanctioned corporate spokespeople and delivered (hopefully) without deviation to a receptive media corps who, in turn, were expected to parrot the messages they've been fed.

Not that this is all gone, but the era of the three-message-plus-talking-point spokesperson may be coming to an end (or, at least, becoming a secondary means of communicating company messages). Consumers increasingly want to deal with corporations on a human level, on their terms, and on their turf. While our corporate spokespeople absolutely need to keep practicing for media outreach, the need for a brand to have spokespeople in social channels can't be ignored.

So what to do? Not every traditional spokesperson has the right stuff to leap into social channels and – warning, social media cliché – join the conversation. The requirements of a BBS community, Google+ Circle, Facebook fans or Twitter followers are quite different from those of a journalist. Journalists aren't typically looking for long-term relationships or dialogue – they're looking for credible sources with stories to tell. Social media communities, on the other hand, want to hear from a human being – not a press release. Someone who tells it like it is, without bludgeoning them with overt corporate messaging. They want advice and information delivered honestly.

And this is the challenge for businesses that realize the power of communities. How do you find a spokesperson that can walk this fine line? How can you help someone build up virtual relationships and not appear a corporate shill? And, most importantly, how do you ensure they are driving conversations that help their companies succeed. As they say, it ain't show friends, it's show business.

Here's some advice for those perched on the horns of this particular dilemma.

1. Determine who the social media spokespeople are

These need to be people who are as comfortable with a blog comment as they are with a quick tweet or creating a new thread in a forum. I feel the best social media spokespeople will have already built up a valid role in these communities. Or if they're heading into new territory, have the time and aptitude to do this properly. The reality is these folks won't typically be the spokespeople of old.

2. Give them a safety net

While one approach is to point a spokesperson at a social media channel and let them go, this is a potential road to ruin. Yes, some people are very comfortable in social media channels and like managing conversations. But – and it's a big but – comfort doesn't equate to success. We expect our new social spokespeople to build relationships, but also help connect the community to our brand. This is where planning, calendar creation, connection with a business' marketing and communications function and on-going coaching become critical.

3. Empower them to get the job done

Companies have for many years feverishly tried to control their brand presence. While many intellectually realize the need for social media interaction, the very thought of putting a spokesperson into the social media wilderness frequently terrifies. This is where organizations need to empower this new generation of spokesperson. Our social media spokespeople need the authority to make decisions and comments in real time. This confidence will often require a change in corporate policy, real-time escalation and prioritization, and a lot of training

Hard work, yes: but the returns are becoming clearer. I don't believe the traditional corporate spokesperson is dead as there will always be a role for people who can represent brands to mainstream media. But those that rely on the media as the sole way of communicating with their stakeholders need to look again at how their critical audiences are making their decisions – and determine if the megaphone alone is the best path forward.

An approach those that want to breach the corporate spokesperson chasm employ is that of building their own communities and employing community managers – those people that keep our shared-interest networks together. That said, one lesson from 2011 – as learned the hard way by companies such as Vodafone and Chrysler – is that managing an online community is not a simple task.

While many companies have created social media presences on Twitter and Facebook with a view to sharing their happy news with keen fans or followers, these channels need editorial direction, management and investment.

A November 2010 Facebook Brand Interaction Study (Beyond, 2010), by my company's sister brand Beyond, told us that the top two reasons for following a brand on Facebook were to find offers and discounts and to demonstrate love for products. But love alone isn't enough to keep people from clicking. Just like a television channel, Twitter and Facebook need programming, new content and interaction – fundamentally a unique reason to keep someone coming back.

Whether the community is for employees, customers, prospective hires or journalists, you can't underestimate the skill required to run this environment. Nor can you ignore the fact that these properties are increasingly the first point of contact for your brand. Ensuring your best people oversee your businesses' most critical online relationships will only become more important as the days go by.

"Who will manage these relationships?" cry time-poor marketing managers. In response, let me tell you a story. You walk into a crowded bar. A group of potential customers stand in a corner. They're talking about your company and your competitors. Interestingly, they're trying to determine which company they should buy from, and each is putting forward solid arguments. So far, it's been a friendly conversation.

You listen for a while. The argument seems to be going your way. What an opportunity! Perhaps it would be a good time for your company to step in and offer its perspective? You can validate any competitive counter claims put forward and have a better offering. But who should talk to them? You need a big hitter. Someone who can get things done. A closer. You reach for your phone . . . and call . . . the office intern?

Far-fetched? I'm not so sure.

It seems this is a scenario playing out in bulletin boards, LinkedIn (www.linkedin.com) Groups, Twitter streams and on Facebook pages all over the world. I guess on face value I should be celebrating the fact that at least these companies have the cojones to talk to their customers. At least they've graduated from paying spammers to crudely ram key messages down their customers' throats and call that social media engagement.

Now don't get me wrong. I have nothing against interns. I think internships are a great way for people starting out in their careers to learn the "ropes". However, their much vaunted digital native bravado doesn't really make them ready for the trenches.

So why would companies put their interns into their client engagements? Are those well-paid sales people too busy to actually sell? Are the PR people too tied up with press releases to spray and pray out to an indifferent press corps? Are your customer support people still answering 800 number calls? Do "resource limitations" mean that the only people left to offer your customers the advice they're looking for aren't drawing salaries?

The answer, I think, is that this is hard. Social media channels are new and largely untested. We've spent the best part of a century convincing our executives that a pile of press clippings equals PR success. And now we want them to do what? Take part in online conversations with complete strangers who may well be 15 years old and not actually in the market for a high end sports car? Are you nuts?

Well, only a little. There's a leap of faith required here. More accurately, a leap that gives us the latitude to participate and learn. We can prove that the conversations are taking place relatively easily. In my home, Hong Kong, forums such as Uwants (http://www.uwants.com/) and Discuss (http://www.discuss.com.hk/) sit in the top ten most visited websites. Facebook is the number one web destination. People are talking online. But we need to make a better case for conversations leading to action. Web analytics is part of the solution and certainly understanding what actions you want people to take on line and determining what can be measured is critical.

Ultimately, though, a company needs the authority to create change. If they genuinely think that online conversations are leading to sales from the wild, then it is time to change the company approach and talk to the very people who want to buy from them. But remember, at no point in the call to action "join the conversation" does it imply "send interns into the conversation".

> The first step – once you understand the online conversation – is to examine people's roles and responsibilities as you prepare to get involved

The first step – once you understand the online conversation – is to examine people's roles and responsibilities as you prepare to get involved. Train the right people for wider roles, but don't throw the baby out with the bathwater.

If the conversations concern customer support, then it makes sense for customer support people to prioritize online in parallel to their regular email or phone roles. If the conversations can be classed as pre-sales, then look at those who manage this function and see how to plug them in. Start small and discreet. Learn from your experience. Rinse and repeat.

Many companies are learning the hard way that social media channels are, well, social. They're often putting these critical customer communications channels in the hands of ill-prepared employees without the support that these vital client facing channels require. Sure, let the interns help. But don't put your brand in the hands of folks who've barely finished high school.

So, hopefully the point is made. Once you have the right people on board as social media representatives, what do you want them to say? And, perhaps more critically, how should they say it?

Mistake number one is to see social as simply another way of pushing your "facile corporate happytalk" (to paraphrase the Cluetrain Manifesto). Social media channels aren't free marketing spam sites. Sadly this perception still exists – and I saw it in action during two recent client meetings in Asia. Client X's head office had forced him to set up a Facebook page – but he'd only go ahead if "there would be NO conversation." Client Y was struggling as his division had developed a cool iPhone app, but the rest of his company (staff numbers in the tens of thousands) didn't care. He couldn't even get a meeting with the client support people.

It is in this environment that we do thankfully find companies that are doing it right. P&G's Social Media Lab programme shows how businesses can use social media and digital channels to fundamentally change their businesses. This programme allows the company to study how customers interact over social media channels. With brand managers understanding these behaviours, P&G has changed the way it communicates – and collaborates – with its customers.

The degree to which P&G understands the practical application of digital influence is shaping its business. Social media's relevance and impact across the breadth of business ecosystems cannot be underestimated. Those companies that have a full appreciation of its ability to infiltrate all areas of their business will inevitably come out on top.

Digital is forcing many enterprises to rethink their business models – from product to sales to customer service to marketing – as it enhances and amplifies their ability to connect with customers, partners, influencers and employees.

Global food and facilities management services provider Sodexho has taken this to heart. They take an integrated approach to recruiting through social media channels using a Facebook page careers blog, LinkedIn group, YouTube channel, Twitter and Flickr. This programme communicates the company's values and work experience while creating ways for prospective employees to interact with the company during the recruitment cycle.

While these businesses are clearly moving in the right direction, they certainly also fall into Moore's early adopters' camp. For many large businesses, getting marketing, sales and customer support to work towards a common goal is a Herculean task. But in this new age, we're asking for more than cross-functional objectives. We want experts to participate in online discussions. This behaviour is alien for the majority of business leaders and we may need a generational shift before we see the right people putting fingers to keyboard and blogging, tweeting or commenting in forums.

I don't underestimate the scope of the change we're talking about. Reshaping the way an organization functions is a seemingly arduous task. Large companies in particular have struggled historically to overcome the business function silos that have frequently evolved as a necessary by-product of their growth. They may intellectually understand that businesses need to participate and change behaviours based on the needs of a new type of consumer – but there's often a gulf between this understanding and the business reengineering required.

In addition, across the business functions there will always be new tools and tactics to influence and connect with customers that force rethinking of frequently entrenched go-to-market models. Businesses also need to get past the scrum over which discipline will "own" the mandate and establish dominance. The change we're talking about is fundamentally bigger than a marketing tug-of-war.

While 2011 was for many businesses a year of social media experimentation, 2012 must be the year of action. Specifically, consolidation on the so-called "Big Four" social media properties of Twitter, Facebook, YouTube and LinkedIn. Not so long ago, these were cloaked in mystery, the playthings of the tech elite. I'd suggest that by the end of 2012 brands will be distinguished if they don't have a presence in these Big Four social media sites – much as brands ten years ago would be called out if they didn't have websites. The Big Four have become mainstream and your customers expect to find you there.

The ultimate prize is to reshape companies for a digital future. The "chasm" is growing but there is still time to make a change. This change must be driven by each business function incrementally, towards a common digital destination. Each function must consider its constituents' needs and begin to engineer digital day-to-day processes around these needs. Those organizations that refuse to take these steps do so at their own peril and face an uncertain future. Those enlightened companies that have a clear, collective sense of the destination and put steps in place to reach it will reap the returns.

Roundup

Want more? See what has been said about this chapter or get involved and discuss it with the author and other readers on our LinkedIn group, find it by visiting http://www.socialmedia-mba.com or search for "The Social Media MBA Alumni".

The concepts put forward so far have hopefully challenged and infuriated you enough to provoke ideas and discussion. You must align your reasoning to that of your business leaders when selling the idea of additional investments into social media.

In the room where social media budgets are agreed the conversation won't be about social media, it will be about business. And those still struggling with the fundamentals will find themselves out of business. It's your job to sell the social vision in a language the rest of the organization will understand.

Once you've got all the internal approvals the next challenge is to get approved by the world outside. What it means to be creative and how to come up with ideas that truly stand out from the crowd will be discussed in the next chapter by Eb Adeyeri.

References

Beyond (2010) The Facebook Brand Interaction Study, Beyond Communications. Available at: http://www.bynd.com/2010/11/24/how-to-build-fb-presence/.

Bughin, Jacques and Chui, Michael (2010) The rise of the networked enterprise: Web 2.0 finds its payday. Available at http://download.mckinseyquarterly.com/the_rise _of_the_networked_enterprise.pdf.

O'Reilly, Tim and Battelle, John (2004) Opening Welcome: State of the Internet Industry. San Francisco, California.

Shiels, Maggie (2010) Facebook, Amazon and Zynga bet on social web, BBC.co.uk, October 21, 2010. Available at: http://www.bbc.co.uk/news/technology-11603380.

Part II

Strategy Development

Chapter 3

What it means to be creative and how to come up with
(and sell) ideas that truly stand out from the crowd

Eb Adeyeri

In short

- How to explore methods for fostering social media creativity and avoid pitfalls.
- Why it's particularly important to emphasize creativity within social media.
- What you can to do take a social media idea from concept to reality.

Overview

In this chapter Eb Adeyeri, Digital Strategist at Ogilvy PR Worldwide, who has worked with clients like Salesforce, Autoglass and Pret A Manger discusses creativity.

Creativity is easy right? Well not necessarily so. Creativity is a buzzword that is thrown around a lot within the PR industry more so with the emergence of social media. However there is still little consideration for what it really means and how to achieve it on a regular basis.

This chapter will look at how to create an environment within which creativity can thrive when running social media campaigns, but also how to get the ideas off the ground in the first place and avoid common pitfalls.

What is creativity?

There are many and various definitions of creativity. Andy Green (whose book I strongly recommend) provides a definition of creativity within the PR function:

> Creativity is something new . . . bringing together two or more different elements in a new context, in order to provide added value to a task.

The best one for me though, from speaking and listening to various people (and this is especially true for social campaigns), can be summed up as simply the history you don't know.

All ideas have been done before. There is really nothing new. It's just a question of finding where it's been done. When developing socially led campaigns it's easy to get carried away with focusing on being the next big thing on Facebook and Twitter. Of course both networks are as good a place to start as any other. But socially led campaigns aren't at all different from the advertising or PR led stunts that have become the main stay of the ad man. At their core, these campaigns start off by defining what the "norm" is and then putting into place a course of action that aims to change the status quo.

The proliferation of media channels and the explosion of social networks means for marketers there is as much a battle for consumers' attention as there is for their money. Attention spans are reduced and, therefore, the imperative to be creative to stand out from the crowd is much greater than ever before.

For PR and marketing professionals, just having the creative idea is never enough. It has to be sold to someone higher up, who often doesn't have a creative mindset. Here it's put through an acid test where it can't be viewed to rock the boat too much. Having an in-depth knowledge of ideas that have been successful previously can help this process. Similarly knowing what hasn't worked can help set the boundaries for the riskier concepts.

Setting the creative boundaries

Risk is central to the process of creativity and this is where social media is a real inhibitor. The crowd has a levelling effect against any tall poppies. To

> With social media, what can be considered a blessing, in that there is little or no structure so ideas can thrive organically, can also be a curse because there is little or no structure so it's very easy to get it wrong.

truly push the parameters, you either need to be psychologically robust, arrogant, mad or all of the above. Creativity is a delicate flower. Critique at too early a stage has destroyed many ideas and much creativity. On social media, criticism is easy, fast and uninhibited. It could be said that the very nature of social media militates against creativity. Social media is for sharing ideas, not conceiving them.

While this is a good thing for companies with a good story to tell (they no longer have to go solely through the prism of the press), it does have its dangers. With social media, what can be considered a blessing, in that there is little or no structure so ideas can thrive organically, can also be a curse because there is little or no structure so it's very easy to get it wrong.

Running a socially led campaign often means the rules have to somewhat be made up on the fly. This is the conundrum facing many who work in the PR and marketing fields. Making things up on the fly is something the industry has been trying to rid itself of for decades in an attempt to be taken seriously by company boards. For this very reason, before embarking on any socially led campaign, it's critical to know what the acceptable boundaries are. There are numerous posts and articles on how to develop a social media strategy, so there's no need to go into details here. Needless to say at the onset of a campaign or initiative everyone involved must know and be comfortable with the rules of the game.

Having a handle on what the tools can or can't do is of course important. (This is probably why I get asked the question, "Is there anything social media wise we can do with that?" on a daily basis.) But it's more important to know the rules of the community or audience you're looking to engage with. I use this analogy a lot, but when you go to a dinner party or bar, you judge the tone or the room and then adapt to it. It's exactly the same with social media.

You need to have a robust social media policy and/or a crisis communications plan before embarking on any social network campaign run. While you can't always accurately predict how the community you're engaging with will react, you must be prepared for the worst-case scenario.

Getting socially creative

For me, inspiring creativity in any campaign is about one thing: invoking a reaction. It doesn't matter what that reaction might be: joy, sorrow, anger, revulsion or hate – controversial but hence the importance of knowing the rules of the game. The worst reaction that a campaign can receive is apathy. Unfortunately most initiatives fall into this bracket because it is easier to resort to the safest course of action.

I often find it ironic that most brands aspire to stand out of from the crowd or their competitors as part of their business plan but often resort to safe, tried and tested methods for their advertising or PR.

Social media has gone someway to changing this approach for many because they see the medium as an opportunity in itself to stand out from the crowd. But as I often say to clients and prospects, social media isn't just about Facebook, Twitter or LinkedIn. It is more of a state of mind: a way of thinking. A commitment to be open about who you are, what you do and the way you go about doing it. Only when a company fully gets to grips with this ethos can it really start to get creative with social media.

Creativity within social networks is about judging the tone of the community and then taking an action that will elicit a response. Taking the analogy further, it's kind of like cracking a joke at a dinner party. If you get it right everyone has a good time and chances are you get invited back. Get it wrong and you're hurled as a social hand grenade.

The creative mindset

It is widely accepted that creativity springs from the right brain. Yet this is seldom used at work. It's no coincidence that the best ideas come to you when you're in a state of relaxation or you brain is "asleep". Be it in the shower, driving, going for a walk (mine is when I've just woken up), the best ideas come when you are in the frame of mind to visualize concepts. Effectively when the left brain is switched off.

Chris Lewis of LEWIS PR (and my former employer) has an interesting theory on this. From his standpoint most creative people are university graduates. Universities are places where the left brain is worshipped for its analytical compare, contrast and analyse function. From an early age young brains are trained to think reductively, to constantly dismiss ideas that don't stand up to a predefined notion of "the norm". However it's just as easy to think synthetically, that is, build up rather than breakdown as a discipline. This is not only a good creative technique, but it's also good for problem solving in business. Synthetic logic can provide an important creative standpoint – that of context. By re-contextualizing an idea we can shed fresh light on it.

Having context is good but it must be managed if any innovation is to get through. The best ideas tend to be the ones that make you a little uneasy. This is where the experience of balancing the left and right brain urges is key. The left brain process can be very destructive. It's so judgemental that sometimes good ideas are dismissed at the point of conception, rather than just left for later review. A good example of this is Post-it notes. 3M were looking for glue and when they found one that didn't stick they dismissed it. However, they later came up with the glue that no-one wanted to stick and post-its were born.

According to Chris, those with highly developed left brains can make the mistake of thinking of themselves as not creative because they are so self-judgemental. In truth anyone with deep intellectual ability can be both. Indeed, the body demands it. This probably goes some way to explain why highly left-brained people tend to drink, take drugs, go mad or become manic sportspeople. The brain craves the balance. This is normally the hallmark of the high achiever – exceptional ability to perform in either left or right brain at will and induce that in other people.

Getting into the groove

Different people have different ways of getting creative. Some listen to music, others prefer complete silence and like to be shut off from everything.

I often think about myself in situations ranging from being manager of a football club and my clients as my team through to being an international spy using espionage to solve a clients campaign problem (what can I say, I love football and James Bond). My point here is that having an active imagination is the foundation for creativity.

Visualizing thinking is a very useful exercise. As human beings we tend to think in images rather than words. Visual brainstorming is a great way to get the creative juices flowing. Whenever I have to come up with an idea for a client, I start by doing lots of reading and analysis of their existing communications channels. I try to get into the mind of all of their stakeholders: from customers through to competitors, employees and journalists. I (in my limited capacity) try to imagine myself as the person on the receiving end of the message.

Over the years I've taken inspiration from Andy Green's book *Creativity in Public Relations* and his five I's process for public relations campaigns, applying the same methods for social media.

In the book, Andy outlines the method for formalizing the creative process into the following: information, incubation, illumination, integration and illustration. This is along the same lines as the Wallas Model (Wallas, 1926).

Information – This is about having all the right information to analyse what the problem being tackled actually is. All too often with social media efforts, the brief received boils down to how to get more fans on Facebook or Twitter. While this might well be a performance indicator of how the campaign is going, it's very rarely the end goal from a business perspective. I'm a firm believer that social media has crucially benefited the PR industry by forcing many practitioners to really get under the skin of a business. Before social networks became a key part of the communications process, it was all too easy for a press release to be the sum output of a campaign. Now the justification required for getting social media type campaigns off the ground means that those responsible have to define their communication problems in very clear terms. To truly be creative with social media you must be clear about the root cause of the problem the campaign is trying to solve.

Incubation – Letting your ideas stew. With the lightning pace of social media, there isn't always time to let ideas fester properly. The pressure is always on to move fast or miss out on the opportunity. In my opinion, this is where many of the social media faux pas of recent years have come from. Numerous ideas are put into action half baked and missing the "killer" ingredient that turns it from "me too" to "award winning."

Illumination – This is all about capturing the ideas before they escape. For me, Evernote is the killer app that helps me capture ideas as they pop into my head. I trawl a lot of sites in the search for ideas but get easily distracted. With the help of Evernote's desktop, iPad and iPhone apps I can pretty much bag and tag a comment, image or video clip as I soon as I come across it for use later on.

Integration – This is the true essence of social campaigns for me. In my experience the best campaigns hardly ever end up being how they were originally planned. They come about from constant evolution and iteration as more information comes to light about what is or isn't possible. The speed at which social media works means this is a crucial part of planning campaigns: the chances of something else capturing the public's attention that could scupper your plan are much greater.

Illustration – Or in simple terms, selling the idea. I'd argue that a large proportion of really good ideas never see the light of day because they aren't sold to the relevant people correctly. How, why, who and when you sell an idea are as important (if not more) than the idea itself. This is even more the case with social campaigns particularly as the industry is very much in its infancy.

One final point on the process of creativity – it is the very stuff of human motivation and self-actualization. Most are unaware; some are interested in it; a few even do it. Fewer still do it and induce others into it. It is one of life's gifts and it can be taught and learned. The great tragedy is that it seldom is.

From the drawing board to making it happen

Pure creativity is where the inexperienced creative starts. With more experience, you realize that you can get higher standards of innovation if you can reassure those to whom you're selling the idea. To this end it's critical to differentiate between pure and applied creativity. If you can't apply it then creativity simply becomes art (which not enough people practice).

If you work in PR or marketing, chances are you're already, in some way, creative. This is only half the story though. Transforming that genius idea into something that you could actually win an award for requires lots of things to come together. As the saying goes, there are a lot of things that are easier said than done. In fact most social campaigns will fail not because they are bad but because there isn't enough time and effort spent on logically thinking through how the concept will work in the real world. The good thing about social media is that, because everything is in the open, you've got the benefit of seeing where others have gone wrong. To coin a popular sporting cliché, having natural talent is only half the way to becoming a success. You also need hard work. The same can be said for creative ideas. You need to work hard to make them a reality.

The key here is to be open and honest about what could potentially go awry, identifying the potential pitfalls that may occur and how to respond if they do.

It's not always fun but I tend to spend a lot of time playing devil's advocate with social campaigns, shooting down what on the face of it often seem like good ideas. While it's impossible to predict every possible outcome, there are ways to work through those ideas that should be left on the drawing board. The best way to approach this is to set out some formulated techniques to separate the wheat from the chaff.

Before embarking on any ideas you need someone on board who will ask:

- How will the idea impact on the company's brand values?
- Who could the idea end up offending?
- Could it land someone in jail?
- Are the risks (and there are always risks) acceptable?
- Will the results be worth the investment or budgets?

All too often with social media, it's tempting to get carried away with trying to create the next Old Spice campaign. This is where having a good old-fashioned media cynic on board to test the idea to destruction is invaluable.

Having fun

My first boss, Andrew Furlong, also used to tell me, "if you can't take a joke you shouldn't have joined". Ultimately all campaigns (whether they are run on social networks or not) are social and about connecting with people. They should be fun to plan and execute. As long as you've got all the checks and balances in place, don't forget to have fun, because if you are then the chances are that others will too.

Roundup

Want more? See what has been said about this chapter or get involved and discuss it with the author and other readers on our LinkedIn group, find it by visiting http://www.socialmedia-mba.com or search for "The Social Media MBA Alumni".

As discussed in earlier chapters, one can argue that social media exposes your brand more than traditional media. The safest way to avoid campaigns backfiring is to have a genuinely creative concept and flexible execution. You can no longer hide behind a somewhat good idea as people will verbalize your shortcomings in full view of other potential undecided prospects.

The future success in the field of social media will be dictated more than anything else by a single, fundamental consideration: giving your fans something to talk about (this will be elaborated further by Alex Yenni in the next chapter).

Chapter 4

Alex Yenni

In short

- Why content is still king, and the role it plays in building your brand.
- How an unknown, small budget spirits brand successfully launched and differentiated itself in a crowded market.
- How to successfully approach your own branded content program.

Overview

In this chapter, New York based Alex Yenni, senior strategist at the multidisciplinary agency SapientNitro, discusses why most social media branding efforts have fallen short because of a formidable hurdle: that between a willingness to *engage* and a willingness to *create*. He explores the opportunity, provides examples and leaves you with a checklist for how to overcome that hurdle.

> Brands are the culture come to life . . . a commercial universe once dominated by the monotony of packaged goods becomes, for better or worse, a world of services and concepts and aspirational identity.
>
> *Michael Wolff, author, brand strategist*

If *social media* was the marketing religion of the late 2000s, then *brand engagement* was its mantra. This new form of digital engagement sought to extend traditional notions of brand identity, and connect brands with consumers both meaningfully and on their own terms. Yet many if not most of those brand efforts have fallen short, and a formidable hurdle remains: that between a willingness to *engage* and a willingness to *create*.

> Content, the digital currency of brand, remains largely an afterthought in even the most well-heeled of social media programmes.

Content, the digital currency of brand, remains largely an afterthought in even the most well-heeled of social media programmes. But one thing is certain – future success in the field of social media will be dictated more than anything else by a single, fundamental consideration: *giving your fans something to talk about.*

What do we mean when we speak of content?

Brand or *branded content* can be thought of as any intentional, brand-authored media used to establish or extend brand identity and affinity. It is used to add context and dimension, to start a conversation, or build loyalty while providing intrinsic value to the consumer independent from that of the product or service. It is most likely to be produced for and featured on brand-controlled properties, but its secondary distribution is often a desired outcome as well. It is *not* advertising in the traditional sense.

What are some examples of branded content? These offerings can be video related (viral, episodic, reportorial), functional (mobile and web applications), auditory (mixtapes, downloads), interactive, gaming-related, editorial, or in the form of an installation or spectacle; really just about anything else that might be used to engage and inspire a consumer base.

On the surface it can be easy to confuse branded content with product placement, but it's important to keep in mind their essential differences. Goodby Silverstein's Gareth Kay clears the air:

> product placement is really about association, linkage and the principles of sponsorship; while the other is about narrative creation – telling and spreading stories, more often than not through film. And this is what creates truly iconic brands.

And while traditional marketing efforts sought to maximize paid channels for distribution, branded content most often relies on organic, peer-to-peer means of distribution. It represents a blurring of the conventional lines between what constitutes advertising and what constitutes entertainment, and is at the very heart of any sound social media strategy.

Explosion in consumption habits

The phenomenon of brand sponsored content has really only taken off with the shifting consumption patterns set about by widespread adoption of both the internet and online social applications (see Figure 4.1). This

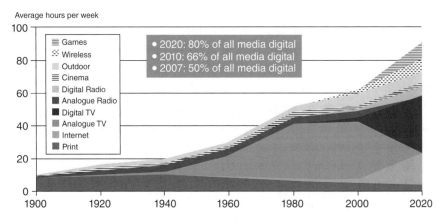

Figure 4.1: Global media consumption per week
Source: Carat ©World Association of Newspapers 2007–2008.

radically redefined communications landscape hasn't markedly decreased the consumption of traditional TV, print and radio, rather it has added an *additional* layer of consumption, a digital layer of arguably more importance.

Why is this so important? Because companies like Facebook have successfully codified and digitally hardwired the most valuable tool in marketing: word of mouth. They have engineered a trusted social context for the sharing of personal information – while simultaneously allowing for the introduction of brand into that conversation.

In-the-flesh social networks – friends, colleagues, family – are now mirrored online, becoming in a sense miniature networks of digital influence. They allow for the seamless, rapid and highly scalable transmission of content and ideas from friend to friend, like-minded user to like-minded user, and individual to network.

It has also created a generation of fickle, expectant and demanding online denizens who are unafraid to engage with brand published content. And while this represents an implicit invitation for the brand to participate in that conversation, it requires a delicate approach, and an approach that adds value. Enter: branded content.

Content wasn't always such a foreign approach

Branded content, a seemingly newfangled medium necessitated by the mechanics of digital distribution, is actually older than you think. In fact a cornerstone of the silver screen, the soap opera, first emerged as radio serials created by the likes of Procter & Gamble and Colgate-Palmolive (manufacturers of detergent, among other things) in the 1920s. They were produced as cultural fodder to help the brands connect with and engender loyalty from stay-at-home wives.

So the use of branded content is not such a departure from traditional marketing approaches, and brand managers needn't feel overwhelmed or like they're recreating the wheel. Rather they should look to their counterparts in entertainment who've pioneered consumer engagement across a variety of mediums and channels, and use it to help inform their *own* brand voice.

New mechanics of distribution

This explosion of social-centric digital connectivity has created a virtual constellation of brand assets across the owned, earned and paid spectrums. For those needing a refresher, *owned* media channels are those that the brand controls – this could mean your Facebook page, your web site, blog or Twitter account. *Earned* media refers to unassisted transfer of brand messaging or content, whether that is through word of mouth, a viral video or a news article. *Paid* media simply refers to those opportunities in which a partner has been paid to feature content, and can take place both in the social space and in more traditional digital arenas (display, search, etc.).

Arraying these assets in a way that makes sense and is both functional and appealing to the digital consumer has necessitated a new approach to brand planning called *connections planning*. Interactive agency Razorfish defines this as,

> [integrating] the work of Account and Brand Planners as well as Media and Analytics, and Social Media. Its core idea is to engage customers where they are and not by putting the customer's media use into the center of attention. Its goal is to use the strength of data-driven marketing activities and integrate all other disciplines to strategically interact with the user and maximize value.

It has also helped create a new role under the digital strategy umbrella, that of content strategist. With an increasingly crowded playing field, *smart* distribution has become an increasingly difficult task for brand teams. Traditionally geared towards earned and paid asset management, marketing groups have seen owned channels emerge from relative obscurity to become a dominant consideration in the planning process. In fact many brands have taken the step of becoming defacto media outlets themselves, curating a rapidly expanding body of proprietary and pop-culture content.

An example: Kanon Vodka

In 2009, Kanon Vodka (see Figure 4.2), a centuries old family-owned vodka distillery in Sweden had a dream: to introduce their superior brand of

Figure 4.2: Kanon Vodka advertisement

vodka to the American market. Flush with ambition but restricted by the massive costs typically associated with this sort of launch, the brand had to make some tough decisions. Should they focus on field sales or paid media: event-based activations or public relations? Through careful consideration and consultation with partner agency The 88, the brand settled on a strategy that would accentuate their unique heritage while amplifying their message among a culturally elite group of taste-makers in key American markets.

"Vodka spirits especially, are like chameleons", said The 88's Harry Bernstein, "they have the unique ability to assume the qualities of whatever context they're placed in". For Kanon, this meant immersing themselves in an edgy, progressive cultural vanguard of party-goers (see Figure 4.3). More importantly, it required the conversion of this on-the-ground social chemistry into a body of unique digital content that could be used to project the brand's vision to an even larger audience. "Endorsement is the oldest tool in advertising, which is why social media campaigns can be so effective if executed authentically. Simply put, we wanted to do social and do it well. And we knew what that would take."

The brand soon embarked on a significant experiential campaign designed to create and curate a body of content to connect consumers with. From edito-

Figure 4.3: Kanon Vodka web site

rial interviews to exclusive video releases, the goal was to distribute material that would appeal to their target group of tastemakers on a gut level. Contrary to the mindset of traditional marketing programmes, there was no explicit call to action. Rather, the brand relied on an implicit association with "cool", on a perception that they knew something that others didn't and an ability to provide vicarious access to that world through the distribution of exclusive content (see Figure 4.4).

To date the project has helped boost distribution of the spirit several times over, including the addition of several new markets. Or, as *Elle* magazine puts it, "for anyone involved in fashion, the phrase 'Kanon Organic Vodka' has become inescapable. Over the past year, Kanon has become like the official sponsor of the young, hip fashion crowd. But how? And why?" Peter Wijk, Kanon's US President, goes on to describe their decision to eschew celebrity sponsorship and paid media campaigns and instead pursue an online strategy of brand created content: "In today's world, that's where people spread their mind. We can do things our way, share things with people and get feedback."

Ultimately, through a combination of sponsored editorial content and event based video and photographic production, coupled with a well thought

THE RAPTURE PERFORMS "HOUSE OF JEALOUS LOVERS"

Everyone agrees that cake is pretty damn tasty... but there's nothing like icing. For us, The Rapture was the icing on our proverbial cake this past weekend. For most people, who've seen the band play in sweaty clubs or huge arenas, seeing them go off on our amazing pool deck whilst jumping into a crystal clear pool was an experience that will pretty much define the summer of 2010.

Figure 4.4: Example of a Kanon Vodka exclusive video release

out utilization of influencer and owned social networks, the brand was able to achieve what traditional advertising could never have bought: authentic influence.

Best practices

The production of branded content (and, more importantly, *content strategies*) takes place on an ever-shifting playing field of experimentation. As social networks grow from adolescence into maturity, brand managers have realized that simply hosting a digital conversation is not enough and that engagement via the standard mechanics of Facebook and Twitter alone do not deliver on the promises touted by their peers. Rather, *owned* media channels must be viewed through the same creative, programmatic lens that one would use to evaluate a traditional advertising campaign of scale.

In his stellar essay, "Why Brands are Becoming Media", Silicon Valley new media guru Brian Solis puts it simply:

> [We] are programing the social web around our brand hub, which requires a consistent flow of engaging and relevant social objects. Social objects are the catalysts for conversations – online and in real life – and they affect behavior within their respective societies.

So what best practices should managers keep in mind when devising compelling, creative and enduring content strategies?

Be authentic – Today's digital consumers are both savvy and fickle. While willing to engage with a brand, brand content has to pass the smell test. Overzealous brand management will render good content inert.

Be up to date – A week is a lifetime, and can mean the difference between 1,000 and 100,000 views.

Create culture – If incapable of creating culture yourself, get behind an effort to enable someone your fans appreciate. You'll be appreciated for it. Don't be a passive participant.

Optimize for your audience – This is "content" after all, not masterpiece theatre. The point of content is to encourage distribution. The key here is achieving the "shareability" factor.

Measure, measure, measure – Consistent measurement and tactical iteration are vital to success.

Have fun with it – This process will undoubtedly be the most creative, flexible and dynamic of all your marketing endeavours. If you're not enjoying the process, it's doubtful any of your fans will either.

Roundup

Want more? See what has been said about this chapter or get involved and discuss it with the author and other readers on our LinkedIn group, find it by visiting http://www.socialmedia-mba.com or search for "The Social Media MBA Alumni".

Content strategist Joe Pulizzi has said, "Nobody has 30 seconds for a brand, but everyone has 30 minutes for a good story." Look at the entertainment sector that has pioneered consumer engagement across a variety of mediums and channels, and use it to help inform their own brand voice.

A great brand experience resonates as well externally as internally and in the next chapter Simon Young will develop this idea of integrating social media within your organization further.

Chapter 5

The entire organization needs to rediscover itself

Simon Young

In short

- Why it's important to create both internal and external engagement.
- How different departments think of social media.
- What Generation C has to do with your social media success.

Overview

In this chapter Simon Young, Partner at New Zealand based engagement consultancy sy-ENGAGE (http://sy-engage.com/), which has worked alongside global clients such as Fonterra and Air New Zealand, explains how we all view social media through the lens of our professional training and background. This is great, and it's also a problem. Social media has the potential to transform organizations into powerhouses of collaboration and creativity. But it won't, unless we reorganize for social media. We need to get over ourselves and our experience, and start to learn the new skills of knowing what we don't know.

"To a hammer, everything looks like a nail."

That saying sums up the attitude many of us take towards social media. We see it through the lens of our professional background. For marketers, social media is a marketing tool. For HR people, social media is an internal communications tool. For IT people, social media is usually an irritant!

The truth is, social media is all those things and more. The challenge lies in bringing all the possibilities together and realizing their potential.

Why I care about this topic

I always used to think being unqualified disqualified me. I was a self-trained radio copywriter who then became a semi-self-trained press release and direct mail writer (and occasional database administrator).

My lack of formal, structured training led me to two things:

1. I always assumed I knew next to nothing, and needed to improve.
2. I didn't know where the boundaries of my specialty were, so I just kept on learning.

Notice how formal training does the opposite of those two things:

1. When our training period is finished, we naturally assume our learning has finished.
2. We know the boundaries of our specialist field, and anything outside that is someone else's problem.

Now I'm not decrying formal, structured education, or saying we don't need it. I'm just noticing the attitude we all tend to take towards it. And perhaps I'm doing the very thing I criticize, using my own point of reference as a general rule for anyone. That's a disturbing thought, but let's put it aside for the moment.

I discovered that naiveté combined with a desire to learn was ideal positioning for working in social media. Not only is the skill set new, the reality is constantly shifting. There is just no longer any room for the "I'm finished learning, now let's start working" attitude.

In a way, it's like the age-old story of the five blind men and the elephant. One man grabs the tail of the elephant, and describes the entire elephant as thin. This makes no sense to the man holding the elephant's ear. "Elephants are flat and flappy," he insists. To the man trying to wrap his arms around the leg, this is utter nonsense: and so on.

It's like that with social media. Tools like Twitter, YouTube and Facebook are just symptoms of a massive social shift that began as long ago as the 1940s.

The shift – in a nutshell

Social media is one symptom of a larger social shift that has three key factors:

- Empowered Consumers.
- The Hunt for Authenticity.
- Co-creation.

These factors didn't start with the internet, they started a long time ago.

Since the end of World War II traditional communities have been breaking down, and virtual communities have been rising up to replace them. Even before the internet, communities of interest such as *Star Trek* fans and Grateful Dead aficionados made a name for themselves. These special interest communities differed from traditional communities in that they were looser in structure, and had a stronger sense of passion.

The arrival of the internet allowed communities to connect, regardless of geography. Case study after case study shows the growing power of virtual communities, sometimes only in existence for a short time, to create social change.

One example of a virtual community is the open source movement. Open source software has done far more than bring free software to market. It's opened up new models of collaboration and co-creation, models that will be refined over time (by many different people) and adopted into the mainstream.

Of course, right now most open source software is still highly idiosyncratic and not easy to use for the average punter. But watch for the principles of open source to make their way into academia, government and business.

What does it look like? A group of peers, from diverse backgrounds, but speaking the same language, working towards a common goal for non-commercial ends.

The growth of virtual communities and new models of collaboration ties in directly with Generation C – the generation that wants an active hand in creating its own future. First identified by Trendwatching.com in 2004, Generation C refers to a generation of content creators who are just as comfortable creating content (blogs, videos, wiki entries) as they are consuming it.

Trendwatching said the C stood for content; Oxford-trained anthropologist Jake Pearce (www.jakepearce.com) disagreed. He saw content as the symptom, not the cause, and sought to explain Generation C by their motivation. His hypothesis: it's about control.

In this light, the icon of Generation C is the iPod, with its ability to create your own playlist. Why, Gen C asks, can we create our own playlist of music, but not our own playlist of other parts of our lives? For example, careers, education, government, banking. Why can't these services be customized and tweaked to an individual's specific preferences?

> It's also important to realize that membership in Generation C depends less on when you're born, and more on your mindset.

It's also important to realize that membership in Generation C depends less on when you're born, and more on your mindset. Some younger people have chosen to eschew a highly customized lifestyle, while older people have enthusiastically embraced the choice and control offered by new technology. Age is irrelevant.

There's a parallel between Generation C and the concept of digital natives, first defined by Marc Prensky as the generation that has grown up with digital technology. However, Generation C also acknowledges "digital immigrants" – people who haven't grown up with the technology, but have adopted the mindset as they've seen it work for them. As such, Generation C is the world's first growing generation, unlimited by the barriers of age.

One of the driving forces of Generation C is the desire to know what's behind the scenes. I believe this hunger for authenticity found expression in technology.

In the 1990s, DVDs replaced videotapes as the standard way to watch a movie outside of the cinema. To differentiate themselves from videotapes, DVDs began to offer special features, often documentaries giving people a glimpse behind the scenes. Soon special features became standard: and for good reason. In a *USA Today* article in 2008, Ken Graffeo of Universal Studios says, "DVD consumers increasingly demand special features that extend and enhance the experience of a movie or TV show."

Around the same time, the reality TV explosion began to hit small screens. Instead of celebrities on the screen, people saw others just like them. Like DVD extras, reality TV often exposed what was "behind the curtain", as shows explored different professions, trades and experiences.

User-generated content has taken this trend further. No longer do people have to audition for someone else's reality show, they can now do everything themselves.

When you create your own content, you look at professionally created content in a different way. You see it from the point of view of a peer, not just a passive consumer. In the same way, today's consumers look at companies and want to know what's going on behind the curtain. How does the system work? How can they win out of that system?

Another facet to the social revolution that has taken and is taking place, is personal branding. In 1998, *Free Agent Nation* by Dan Pink predicted a future USA where more and more people turn to the freedom of self-employment, empowered by the internet.

The following year Tom Peters' book *A Brand Called You* echoed some of the themes of Pink's book, looking at how people can cultivate their own personal brand.

Ten years later, the mass exodus to self-employment hasn't happened, but personal branding is no less important. Once again, social media has driven this existing trend. Everybody who has created a social network profile has had to make a branding decision. Choosing a photo, trying to describe oneself in a few sentences, are all marketing activities previously reserved for organizations and celebrities.

Organizations have taken two different responses to this. Some have embraced the potential of personal branding, recognizing that their brand is most often delivered by the individuals who work for them, and empowering individuals to build individual relationships with customers. For example, online retailer Zappos has many of its employees on Twitter, serving customers in a holistic way, being themselves as well as representing the Zappos brand.

Other organizations have either ignored personal branding entirely or tried to stamp out individuality in favour of adhering to brand guidelines.

The collision of personal and corporate branding brings up two thorny questions:

- If companies allow staff to build their own personal brand, what happens to the company brand? Does it become inconsistent?
- If companies allow staff to build their own personal brand, won't they take customers with them when they leave (and, particularly in this day and age, they will leave)?

These questions – and their disconcerting lack of answers – might seem a good reason for companies to actively discourage or at least ignore personal branding. But doing so is very dangerous, for two reasons.

One, customers seek authenticity and humanity in their transactions. That doesn't necessarily mean they want to queue in line to see a bank teller instead of using an ATM, but the experience economy means that when they do interact with another person, they want it to be meaningful and memorable.

Two, staff – particularly Generation Y and Generation C – want to work somewhere that lets them express themselves. Somewhere that lets them meet the needs near the top of Maslow's hierarchy of needs, including self actualization.

On both sides, there's a hunger for authenticity, driven by the experience economy, the rise of Generation C, and peripherally, corporate social responsibility, which demands that businesses be more than just resource users and profit creators.

So we've described the elephant – the virtual communities, Generation C, empowered (and curious) consumers, and the desire consumers have to create their own destiny. Now where are the blind men?

The blind men – aka our training and backgrounds

Let's look at how different departments look at the world – and, therefore, how they treat social media.

Marketing

Marketers – and especially the agencies that serve them – tend to divide in one of two directions: the *branders* and the *direct marketers*.

The branders' argument basically goes:

> The most important factor in a buying decision is the emotional connection between brand and consumer. Therefore, we must appeal to underlying human emotions and seduce, lull, entertain and dazzle our consumers into loyal behaviour.

When it comes to measuring brand awareness and the loyalty that (we hope) follows, marketers have traditionally relied on market research, sales figures and a whole heap of assumptions bringing them together.

Branders use TV and newspaper advertising, and often go for the biggest reach. Their role models are iconic consumer brands and the entertainment industry.

The direct marketing crowd's mantra, meanwhile, is:

> Hold your advertising accountable. Measure everything. Constantly improve your marketing by measuring it and dropping the activities that don't deliver results.

Traditionally direct marketing has measured a correlation with sales, or some step towards a sale (for example, requesting more information, subscribing to an email newsletter or entering a competition).

Direct marketers look at social media quite differently from branders. They see a series of actions that can be measured (often in quite some detail). Where brand awareness is long term and big-picture focused, direct marketing is short term and focused on detail.

Direct marketers know the truth of Peter Drucker's phrase, "You can't manage what you can't measure." Once seen as a poor cousin to the marketing profession relegated to cheap and nasty-looking things like mail order catalogues and infomercials, accountable marketing has been increasingly popular in recent years, because of harder financial times and also the ability of online channels to measure many more interactions.

For branders and direct marketers alike, social media seems to provide some hard measures where once there was only highly educated guesswork. Now you can know for sure how many people are following you on Twitter, or liking your brand on Facebook. Can't you?

Sadly, no. Opting-in by liking, following or subscribing is not a guarantee that your audience will even see your brand. It only increases the odds. In fact, a more important measure than brand awareness these days is brand engagement. "Likes" and sharing of content gives some indication of engagement, but it's not a bulletproof formula.

Thankfully, branders are intuitive thinkers. They know that, as Einstein said, "not everything that counts can be measured; not everything that can be measured counts."

The new frontier for brand awareness is engagement. Engagement with a brand often involves conversation – an element missing from old-style brand awareness. It includes the consumer having a voice and also hearing the voice of other consumers. It doesn't mean the brand abdicates its leadership position. Branding has never been completely democratic. People are attracted to a brand because it stands for something. They want a voice, but they also want the brand to have meaning.

The new frontier for direct marketers is applying what has been learned to all aspects of the organization, not just selling stuff. In fact, this is what great direct marketers have always done – created their marketing campaigns and programmes in such a way that, even if the campaign doesn't achieve the desired result, the company still learns every time. Learning turns to insights, which in turn become new product features and offerings. Measurable marketing can become an innovation powerhouse.

PR/communications

PR practitioners and business communicators often have a much more ambiguous brief than marketers. Instead of driving sales, communicators are focused on balancing the needs of various "publics" and ensuring the right people get the right message at the right time.

Communicators measure their efforts by sheer reach (for example, being featured in major media), and by the accuracy of the reporting about their organization from mainstream media and the public.

Risk management is another aspect of communicators' success measurements. The best communicators spend half their time keeping bad news stories about their organization out of the spotlight, while emphasizing the positive.

For communicators, social media has been an invaluable tool to *become* their own media. Traditionally public relations (or specifically media relations) has strongly relied on others (reporters, editors) to deliver their messages. While they often have nothing to worry about (with busy or lazy reporters sometimes reprinting press releases word for word and presenting it as news), having their own channel is very important when it comes to contentious or complex issues.

Communicators face a similar challenge to direct marketers: what to say in between the strategic bits. Direct marketers are used to making an offer. Communicators are used to addressing an issue – whether it's proactive (e.g. a product launch) or reactive (e.g. a crisis). These things are interesting and relevant for consumers, but they are not enough to sustain an ongoing relationship with the customer.

This is where communicators and direct marketers can learn from branders. Branders know that consumers connect not with products and offers, but with stories and feelings. The best brands are carriers of a story larger than the product or service offered; something that reflects a reality that the consumer wants to be part of.

No-one would watch a TV channel that only played ads, would they? (OK, no-one outside the advertising industry.) Similarly, social media channels that are exclusively geared towards offers or crisis communications are unlikely to appeal to people. A quick survey of the most subscribed channels on YouTube shows that people connect with people, not products.

The greatest opportunity for communicators in social media is to become the media, telling stories that resonate with their audiences and, better still, involve them.

Customer service

Another department that has found itself dragged into social media is the call centre. Customer service people are all about solving problems, and social media has given them many new sources for problems to solve.

Following the lead of companies like Dell, companies have dedicated resource to social media as a customer service channel. The big difference is the public nature of social media. It's like having a call centre conversation broadcast live on TV.

That's why talent has become very important. In any call centre there are top performers, and companies are starting to see the need to put those top performers where they will shine the most – on social media.

The trouble lies in the key measurements for customer service. A call centre is about solving problems quickly. Efficiency is paramount. While it's great to solve customer problems quickly, it's important to realize that with social media the goal is to continue that ongoing relationship.

So customer service needs to take its existing metrics (for example, time to answer a query) and collaborate with communications and marketing (who want to ensure the conversation continues in a positive direction). Together, these three departments can then move on to co-create with the customer.

Information technology

The information technology (IT) department is usually at the extreme end of the adoption spectrum: enthusiastic early adopter of social media, or staunch barrier against it. It usually depends almost entirely on the individual in charge.

IT is concerned about security and efficiency. What keeps them up late at night is the personal/professional boundary that social media seems to be blurring. It presents many threats (e.g. employees leaking confidential information, inadvertently downloading viruses, etc.) but it also presents many opportunities (e.g. employees advocating strongly on behalf of the company online, with clear guidelines). IT needs to collaborate with communications and human resources to ensure this happens intentionally, and not just piecemeal.

Human resources

Human resources (HR) is concerned with recruitment (and that's where they often see opportunity in social media) and compliance. They can understand both the risk and opportunity of more information being available to more people online.

HR is also concerned (or should be) with staff engagement. Social media offers an outstanding opportunity to engage members of staff by letting their voices be heard. In a recent client engagement, we encouraged staff from around the world to send in videos of themselves – an audition of sorts (the prize was producing a global documentary). While the prize was compelling, so was the experience of seeing and hearing the unfiltered, unedited voices of their workmates. As the competition winner told me, "We're used to hearing from the CEO or the chairman, but this campaign was different . . . we were seeing each other!"

Using social media for internal engagement achieves several aims:

- Greater engagement, communicated by the company's willingness to give staff a voice.
- A test case for the use of social media externally.
- Talent spotting, to find good communicators within the company who can potentially represent the company in future public social media efforts.

Finance

Finance as a department only understands two things: money saved and money earned. Social media can do both, *if* all the other departments learn together how to use it.

How it all fits together

In a recent workshop, we created a social media strategy for a fictitious company. We divided up attendees into the separate departments, and asked them to develop objectives and strategies for their department.

The fictitious company sounded like a paradise. Marketing knew they were supposed to support customer service, service knew they needed to look after IT. Because they were starting from scratch, there was mutual respect and a common focus on the company's success.

Unfortunately, the reality is often different. Departments and individuals have historical baggage and conflicting goals. The good news is that the same process of building alliances and co-creating a solution together happens inside first, then outside. The right way to engage in social media is to co-create with your audience. So however messy the process seems at the time, think of the internal exercise as practice for the future we now all share.

Roundup

Want more? See what has been said about this chapter or get involved and discuss it with the author and other readers on our LinkedIn group, find it by visiting http://www.socialmedia-mba.com or search for "The Social Media MBA Alumni".

A company that wants to engage external audiences in social media needs to start by engaging internal audiences. How to do that is the subject of entire books,[1] but here are a few tips that apply to both internal and external engagement:

- Acknowledge the baggage. Never be silent about the elephant in the room, otherwise everything else you say will not be heard effectively.
- Let everyone's voices be heard. We begin workshops on social media by asking the room for their one-word perceptions of social media, positive and negative. When people know that their voice is heard, they are ready to listen and try something new.
- Be a "ragtag" leader who can bring people together to co-create, even (especially) if they're not in your department. Embrace each party's ambitions and goals, and be the one who facilitates a combination of those goals into a common overall goal.

As a lot of people look for opinion guidance from peers, one negative comment can set the tone for many more to follow. This is explored further in the next chapter by Ged Caroll where he asks you to consider the intent of your target audience's online journey.

---

[1] For example, *Silos, Politics and Turf Wars* by Patrick Lencioni and *A Sense of Urgency* by John Kotter.

Chapter 6

Why looking beyond demographics makes sense in digital marketing and how to do it

Ged Carroll

In short

- What is wrong with the traditional demographics-based planning model?
- How to think of your target audience for best results.
- Why you have no time to lose.

Overview

Changes in consumer behaviour that challenged traditional marketing segmentation models have been written about since the mid-1990s and campaign planning has had to adapt with it.

In this chapter by Ged Carroll, based in Hong Kong and Director Digital Strategies at Ruder Finn, an agency with clients such as 3M, Weight Watchers and Johnson & Johnson, discusses why online and more recently social media has changed the way consumer demographics should be considered.

Identities have become more fluid so how do you plan campaigns? A key part of the answer to this conundrum is thinking about campaign planning by considering the intent of a user's online journey.

What's wrong with the traditional demographics-based planning model?

It may not feel like it at times with the banking crisis and rising fuel prices but consumers in the developed world have never had it so good.

Consumers now enjoy much more economic power than previous generations. With this economic power has come much more choice. Technologist and author Kevin Kelly, whilst promoting his book *What Technology Wants*, talked at The Churchill Club about how a medieval king of England has his possessions counted as a way of calculating the total value of the country and the total came to some 2,800 objects; but by contrast Kelly worked with one of his children to do the same audit of their house and stopped at 10,000 objects (Fora.tv, 2010).

So on one scale of measurement consumers today are likely to be richer than former kings of England. For a more suburban example, ask yourself since when has cheesecake been a basic necessity for the average consumer? Yet cheesecake and ground coffee are part of at least one well-known UK supermarket's basics range. This massive expansion of supermarket offerings has been going on since the 1980s.

At the other end of the consumer goods marketplace, the luxury sector has seen its clients come from a wider social group than would have previously been the case. All of this choice has happened due to industrialization, technological progress, shipping containers and economic globalization. This all means that for many goods income and class are no longer as effective in determining whether a consumer in the developed world will purchase or not.

> All this choice and economic power has allowed researchers to see new psychological phenomena like *choice blindness*.

All this choice and economic power has allowed researchers to see new psychological phenomena like *choice blindness* (New Scientist Online, 2009). Societal changes have also changed what we do and when we do it; for instance fewer people are getting married, there has been a rise in the number of single-person households and adults have generally been behaving younger for longer. This means that a lot of the traditional assumptions that came with segmentation are no longer as robust a model as they have been in the past.

By the mid-1990s marketing thinkers were trying to reframe segmentation in terms of tribes to match post-modern thinking with marketing concepts (Cova, 1996). Yet it could be argued that even the model of tribes fails to deal adequately with the increasingly fluid identities that had developed.

Online has extended the amount of choice available to consumers even further, with search engines providing access to billions of web pages, images, video and electronic documents. In order to match this explosion in choice, worldwide logistics services have filled the gap to provide cost-effective delivery services. This has resulted in a complex distribution of products and services called The Long Tail, which demonstrates the relationship between "blockbuster" products or services and more niche offerings (*Wired* magazine online, 2004). In addition, most consumers in the developed world now have some sort of near-universal payment systems such as MasterCard, Amex, Visa or PayPal that allow them to capitalize on the choice.

Whilst consumers have shaped the direction of online and supporting services, the web has in turn shaped consumer behaviour, which is continually changing and adapting as new web services come along. Just in the past few years we've seen consumers go from placing the most trust in "people like us" to focusing again on experts as thought leaders, as Facebook redefined what it meant to be a friend (Edelman Editions, 2011).

Consumers now enjoy wider, looser social networks than they did prior to the web. It is even thought that online social networks are adversely affecting how we feel about ourselves (Jordan, Monin, Dweck, Gross, John and Lovett, 2011).

Social media researcher danah boyd found that young people treat their online identities as transient things that they can throw away or start-up to reinvent themselves with great ease (danah boyd | apophenia, 2007). Profile content is left behind and recreated anew when moving social platforms or creating a new identity, thus making these consumers harder to fit into a marketing segment.

Why intent?

In some ways using audience intent instead of demographics is about taking marketing back to its roots.

Modern, or to be more accurate, industrial consumer marketing had its roots in the consumer boom that came at the end of the first industrial age. This was driven by the likes of Lever Brothers (now part of Unilever) with their Sunlight and Lifebuoy soaps. James and William Hesketh Lever founded Lever Brothers. William Lever is now more famous to marketers than consumers, as he is often credited with the famous quote "I know half my advertising isn't working, I just don't know which half" – a problem that focusing on the customer intent helps to address.

Prior to this consumer boom, shopkeepers and merchants were an intimate part of their communities; they had a good understanding of their immediate environments, local customs, and they knew their customers on a personal level so understood their intent – but probably didn't conceptualize it in that way!

Mass-production met and began to exceed demand, globalization accelerated the subsequent age of consumerism, but marketing as a discipline has taken longer to catch up as it continued to shoe-horn consumers into demographic segments.

From an ethical standpoint there is something to be said about treating people as individuals rather than market segments; it comes down to that very human need for respect. It helps to engender an organization mindset that will be more customer-focused and less likely to be in the middle of a social media storm due to consumer dissatisfaction.

Intent as the new demographic

We tend to envisage intent using an illustration, shown in Figure 6.1, that we call the intent process.

The process starts with an individual's intent, whether it is to break up a long writing session by finding something amusing to watch on YouTube as a three-minute diversion, search for information or a solution to a problem, communicate, impress the world with their creativity or use the web as a form of DIY therapy to get things off their chest. From a marketer's perspective it is about determining the intersection of audience intent with their business goals. If there is a point of intersection then the brand has some utility to the

Intent into interaction

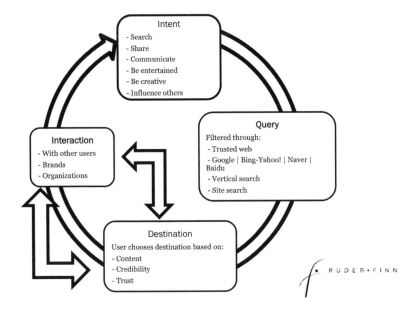

Figure 6.1: The intent process

consumer. Put into online marketing, efforts are more likely to be rewarded by a customer interaction.

This intent drives the next stage in the process: query.

Whilst many digital marketing efforts focus on search engines, there are numerous other query points to consider, for example:

- Their trusted web: friends on social bookmarking sites, posting a question on their own Facebook wall for people to come back to them, an open question to their Twitter friends, or questions on Q&A sites like Quora, Korea's Naver or dedicated forums.
- Site search: for instance looking up a book on Amazon, or a subject area on Wikipedia, IMDb (The Internet Movie Database) for film-related trivia.
- YouTube: not only the world's largest video site, but also the western world's second largest search engine.
- Vertical search: for instance Google Scholar or Scirus for scientists and academics.

Query results are based on content and conversation, and can be both influenced and shaped. There are various tactics that the marketer can deploy to influence or shape query results to help intercept the customer, for instance pay-per-click advertising, the creation of site content, social search optimization, linking strategies and search engine optimization.

The query leads to a destination, which they will evaluate in terms of trustworthiness and quality of the content. They may choose to look at several online destinations depending on how detailed and expensive the decision may be. In terms of a digital marketing perspective the destination offers a second chance to intercept the customer. This could be done by creating destinations, conducting blogger or community outreach to facilitate quality content or engaging via a social networking platform.

In the case of social networks it answers one of the most common questions that organizations ask digital marketers, which usually goes along the lines of "I have <insert number> of followers on <usually Facebook or Twitter> social network, what do I do next?"

Ideally the organization should look to deliver valuable messages and shareable experiences that relate directly to the user's intent; this can spark customers to extend the reach of a message through their own social networks.

Interaction on the destination site is key; one group that does this particularly well is the pre-sales team for Vodafone UK who can be found on Twitter at @vodafoneukdeals. It is worthwhile following them to see how they operate their Twitter account.

So you end up with three points at which you can intersect with the consumer based on their intent (see Figure 6.2).

The three ways of intercepting the consumer are:

- intercepting the query;
- working with, or creating destination sites; and
- interacting directly with the customer, or empowering community members with suitable useful information to interact with the customer.

The precise mix of these tactics should be determined by an understanding of the initial intent.

Intent into interaction

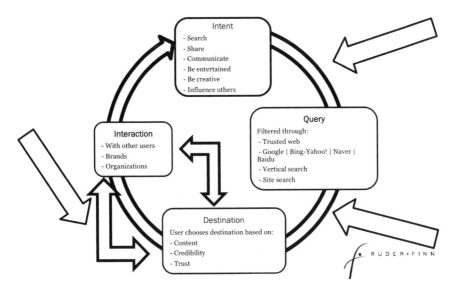

Figure 6.2: The three points of interception with the consumer

The customer's level of prior experience or domain knowledge is going to affect their path from intent to interaction.

Let me illustrate this by using myself as an example: I am a bad photographer, but I quite enjoy it and keep a visual diary on Flickr. I eventually decided to move from a point-and-shoot camera to a digital SLR camera. I used Google to find articles on photography, which helped me to think about what I actually want in a camera.

I found additional links from my friend Dave who is a talented software engineer and amateur photographer. I soon realized that lenses are a more critical part of the purchase decision than the camera body itself. You may change the camera body but the lens will do you far longer; also lenses are expensive so once you commit to a platform it is hard to move. A search on eBay revealed that Pentax tended to have the cheapest second-hand lens available.

I then read reviews of Pentax cameras to work out which model would best suit me. Once I knew the model I then looked at price comparison sites to find the best value offer currently available.

What we see in this example is the query process, a number of destinations and interactions as my intent changed from gaining knowledge, to working out a brand preference, to honing down a purchase choice by deciding on a particular camera and calculating what bundle of accessories I wanted based on the overall value offered by the suppliers.

Quite unintentionally, I ended up buying the camera from the online outlet of the camera shop below our office, which added an additional level of convenience.

Technology moves on and pretty soon I was ready for a new camera. This time the process that I went through looked quite different. I knew I wanted a Pentax digital SLR; I just wasn't sure which one I wanted.

I went to sites that I had previously bookmarked and read the camera reviews, made a decision and then used shopping comparison sites to try and find the best deal. My heightened experience level in this case meant that my journey from intent to buying the camera was much shorter than the first time. It would have been pointless for a rival camera manufacturer like Canon or Nikon to try and persuade me to purchase one of their cameras, as this would have clashed with my intent as a customer, partly because the Pentax system of lenses provides a powerful lock-in to me as a consumer. Getting me to move brands would only work if:

- I lost my entire collection of camera lenses, so I was starting from scratch again.
- I had an awful experience with my current camera that I didn't want to go through again.

This also shows how focusing on the consumer intent helps marketers to cut down on wasteful campaign activity that wouldn't deliver results for the organization.

So how do I find out about intent?

The bad news has been that lazy digital marketing based on "buckets" of audiences, whether they are tribes or demographically defined segments, isn't the best way forward. However, much of the information needed to understand intent is either available online or resides within an organization.

To start things off we have set up a site at intentindex.com where we share top-line research results about the intent of consumers going online. This shows seven main categories of intent that we have identified:

- Shop
- Learn
- Have fun
- Socialize
- Personal expression
- Advocate
- Do business

Clicking any of these categories allows you to drill down a bit further into the data. We hope to re-run this on a regular basis so feel free to check back for new or updated data points.

Sources of data inside an organization include:

- Customer services records and inbound enquiries.
- Customer surveys (particularly the qualitative data collected as part of Net Promoter score questionnaires.
- Field sales and service reports in the case of business-orientated organizations.

All of these sources offer a treasure trove of information. But if this information isn't available, do a small incentivized survey of the organization's clientele and web visitors.

Going back through web analytics data can help you find where audiences are coming from, for example possible sources of queries or conversations that are relevant to the organization's brand. What key words are audiences using to find the organization's website?

A key part of planning a digital marketing programme is conducting an online audit; this usually looks like a measure of influence of the sites or online sources and is some sort of sentiment analysis. But an overlooked aspect of this is studying the context of the comments and content produced. This audit provides a wealth of information if you view it from the perspective of an online ethnographer and look for clues as to the likely user intent.

What are the frustrations emerging from social media interactions? These frustrations can usually be tied back to an original intent.

What can you learn from online artefacts? Are there pictures or videos taken of the product or service in use by customers? For instance there is a whole sub-genre of foodies who obsessively document their restaurant meals and own efforts on the Flickr photo-sharing site to entertain their friends and fellow food fans.

Digital marketing and intent

Ultimately using intent as the new demographic in campaigns is about gaining more benefit from less marketing activities. As an industry we are often too task-orientated; wanting to do things, focusing on outputs in terms of "digital embassies" across social platforms or creating our own platforms to reach audiences, engage consumers and message delivery.

Intent as the new demographic is about spending more time thinking about programmes from a consumer point of view, what is likely to be useful and where are the appropriate points for the brand to intercept the individual during their online journey? Or, as William Hesketh Lever would have put it, knowing which half of my digital marketing isn't working, and doing something about it.

Roundup

Want more? See what has been said about this chapter or get involved and discuss it with the author and other readers on our LinkedIn group, find it by visiting http://www.socialmedia-mba.com or search for "The Social Media MBA Alumni".

While digesting this perspective, try to apply the thinking to your organization. Why not start off by having conversations with colleagues asking the following questions:

- What kind of data and insights do you currently have that could be used as a starting point to develop a customer intent-driven campaign?
- What actions would you like your users or customers to take as a result of your campaign?
- How does the online presence you currently have fit with your customer's intent? How could it be modified to align their intent with your desired user action?

Combine the conclusions from above with the insight in the next chapter by Tim Hoang and you can take the next step of identifying influential people that can create buzz around your product or service.

References

Cova, B. (1996) What postmodernism means to marketing managers. *European Management Journal*, **14**(5), 494–499.

danah boyd | apophenia (1 January 2007) ephemeral profiles (cuz losing passwords is common amongst teens) http://www.zephoria.org/thoughts/archives/2007/01/01/ephemeral_profi.html [Accessed 30 July 2011].

Edelman Editions (2011) Trust Barometer 2011. Available at http://edelmaneditions .com/2011/01/trust-barometer-2011 [Accessed 30 July 2011].

Fora.tv (2010) Kevin Kelly What Technology Wants presentation at The Churchill Club [video online] http://fora.tv/2010/11/03/Kevin_Kelly_What_Technology _Wants [Accessed 30 July 2011].

Jordan, A.H., Monin, B., Dweck, C.S, Gross, J.J., John, O.P. and Lovett, B.J. (2011) Misery Has More Company Than People Think: Underestimating the Prevalence of Others' Negative Emotions *Personality and Social Psychology Bulletin* (January 2011).

New Scientist online (18 April 2009) Choice blindness: You don't know what you want by Lars Hall and Petter Johansson. Available at http://www.newscientist.com [Accessed 30 July 2011].

Wired magazine online (October 2004) The London Tail by Chris Anderson. Available at http://www.wired.com/wired/archive/12.10/tail.html [Accessed 30 July 2011].

Chapter 7

Tim Hoang

In short

- How the traditional notion of "influencer" may not be as important as many believe.
- How to plan and manage more successful campaigns.
- How you can capture the easily influenced.

Overview

In this chapter Tim Hoang, Senior Digital Consultant at Cohn & Wolfe with clients like McDonalds, Nike and Ford, discusses how much of the talk in marketing and social media is based on the influentials theory, partially because it is easy to justify to ourselves and our clients, and everyone else seems to buy into it. However, there appears to be an ongoing argument as to the plausibility of these small groups of influential people – influentials – who are able to cause a revolution by having a vague combination of charisma, popularity and a penchant for helping others.

Why the easily influenced may be more important than influential

It's ironic that while every social media and communications expert continues to argue about what the definition of an "influencer" actually is, many continue to sell campaigns to clients with the crux of activity focused on targeting this unidentified group of individuals.

There is also the issue of the plausibility of this small group of influentials being able to cause a revolution simply by having a hazy combination of charisma, popularity and an inclination for helping others.

However, by looking at how messages actually spread through different groups of people, we can see how big a role these influentials actually play in creating trends and influencing the population.

The traditional influencer model

For any business, identifying influential people is one of the most important activities to creating buzz around your product, service or offering. As Malcolm Gladwell describes in his book *The Tipping Point*, these people, with their charismatic personalities, ability to connect networks and interest in helping people make informed decisions, can create movements ranging from an increase in sales of a certain type of footwear to the spread of diseases.

Those working in the communications industry are well practiced in targeting influencers with huge investments made in persuading them to endorse a brand or product. The idea of identifying this small group of people or opinion leaders in order to spread corporate messages to everyone else is highly endearing and has been the bedrock of the communications industry since Paul Lazarsfeld introduced his Two-Step Flow Communications Model in 1944 and subsequently expanded on it with Elihu Katz in 1955 (Two Step Flow Theory, 2004).

The rise in the use of social media has further complicated the situation – anyone with an idea can create a blog and publish it to the web and those with even shorter attention spans can update their friends via Twitter: everyone, it seems has the potential to be an influencer.

Analytic tools are released regularly purporting to have the ability to evaluate one's level of influence – with Klout being the tool on everyone's lips at the time of writing. These all rely on an arbitrary formula that tries to make sense of a range of inputs such as number of Twitter followers, comments on a blog or frequency of blog posts. However, the question we have to ask is: How can this finger in the air mathematics actually equate to "influence" when no one has even come to an agreed explanation of what being influential is?

Influencer versus network structure

When one thinks of a trend started by an influential, one would imagine the content (for the sake of argument let's assume it's a video) is passed on from person to person until it hits an influencer and suddenly spreads to everyone else due to their high connectivity and persuasiveness – and *voila*! Men start wearing cardigans without a hint of irony. Marketers would simply locate these influencers, give them the content and watch the income roll in.

Duncan Watts, a principal research scientist at Yahoo! Research has a different take on the topic. In his research paper, "A Simple Model of Global Cascades on Random Networks", Watts discusses how the role of influencers may not be as important for the spread of trends as the actual structure of the connections in a network of people.

His research investigated networks of "people" with varying levels of connectedness and different levels of "susceptibility" (i.e. how likely they are to adopt a new idea or try a new product). When networks were fragmented and people not well connected, those with high connectivity (i.e. the influencers) were more likely to be the catalyst for spreading ideas. However, these trends remained localized as the ties connecting different groups of people were infrequent or did not exist – the trends spread, but only within a small clique of people. This could explain the insular, localized nature of messages spreading within the social media "bubble", where highly connected and influential individuals can cause a burst of conversation among their followers, but rarely does it permeate into the mainstream.

In more connected networks, however, the impact of the highly connected individual is less significant. When everyone is highly connected, the relative influence of a single person is not as important as in a network where people have fewer connections.

The reason for this is related to the variable in the experiment that gave each "person" a different level of susceptibility to adopting a new idea. When people change their minds about a topic, they rarely do so in isolation, nor do they simply copy the first person they hear the information from. Instead, it might take any number of people to convince them to change their behaviour. This "tipping point" is also known as the threshold.

Thresholds and decision making

There are a number of pressures which force or encourage a person to make a decision. These can include conforming to social pressures from friends or colleagues to financial pressures for adopting the latest technologies. Change in behaviour is not as simple as being exposed once to a new idea, there are combinations of factors that affect why people change how they think or feel about a particular subject.

The threshold is the point at which a stable state changes. For example, water has a temperature threshold before it boils, you will have a threshold for the number of beers you can drink before you need to use the toilet or for the number of packed tube trains you let go past in the morning before braving it and squeezing on.

Thresholds have a similar meaning in relation to decision making and creating trends and social norms.

Every one of us has a threshold that determines how long it will be before we change our behaviour. In terms of social persuasion, your threshold is the number of people who are influencing you at the time you "change" and can be written as a fraction or probability. An example I've used previously to explain how thresholds work is that of the smacking of children. Very simply, if more people in your social group smack their child then you will be more likely to do so (or certainly believe it to be more acceptable). The percentage

> To make an idea trend, the role of the highly influential is not as significant as some would have you believe. In fact, the catalyst for the spread of an idea across a whole network is likely to be started by someone who is not particularly "influential".

of people in your network at the point you change your beliefs or ideology is your threshold for this particular issue.

Therefore, the more people you are connected to, the more people are needed to make you change your opinion. This is why highly connected people in highly connected networks will find it more difficult to influence an individual due to the number of other people also trying to voice their opinion. To make an idea trend, the role of the highly influential is not as significant as some would have you believe. In fact, the catalyst for the spread of an idea across a whole network is likely to be started by someone who is not particularly "influential".

Diffusion and the spread of information

Watts' research is based on the assumption that social ties are one of the most important factors in persuasion. The two-step communication model similarly assumes that while the mass media increases awareness, it is in fact interpersonal communications that persuade one to adapt or change behaviour. During the process of adoption, when enough people change their behaviour and therefore influence their network, random activity of unrelated events becomes seemingly more predictable as a kind of self-organization takes over. The point at which this occurs is known as the network's critical mass, where suddenly the momentum of the adoption rate fuels its own growth. Table 7.1 shows the cumulative rate of adoption in a population.

Critical mass of a trend can be found at the point where the acceleration of adoption rate first decreases – people are still adopting the idea but at a slower rate than before (the first inflection point of the table). At its critical mass, it can be assumed that the idea will have been adopted by between 10 and 20 per cent of all the people who will eventually adopt the idea (it is no surprise to find that innovators and early adopters and opinion leaders

Table 7.1 Cumulative rate of adoption in a population

Time	Cumulative number of fans	Cumulative % of fans	Adoption Rate	Acceleration
0	6	2.68	5	4
1	15	6.7	9	5
2	29	12.95	14	22
3	65	29.02	36	17
4	118	52.68	53	−31
5	140	62.5	22	−5
6	157	70.09	17	−7
7	167	74.55	10	−1
8	176	78.57	9	−1
9	184	82.14	8	−3
10	189	84.38	5	−2
11	192	85.71	3	4
12	199	88.84	7	0
13	206	91.96	7	−5
14	208	92.86	2	−1
15	209	93.30	1	1
16	211	94.20	2	1
17	214	95.54	3	0
18	217	96.88	3	−1
19	219	97.77	2	−2
20	219	97.77	0	1
21	220	98.21	1	−1
22	220	98.21	0	2
23	222	99.11	2	−2
24	222	99.11	0	2
25	224	100	2	−2

Source: http://www.mitsue.co.jp/english/case/concept/img/02/fig1.gif

represent 16 per cent of consumers and fall into this range). Theoretically then, we can assume that the total number of eventual adopters will be five to ten times the number of people at the point of critical mass.

A recent Facebook fan page I created for a client can help illustrate this point. Figure 7.1 shows the rate at which fans joined the page.

In the table, at Time 3 the total number of fans is 29. Therefore, we could estimate the number of eventual fans to be between 145 and 290 (the mean

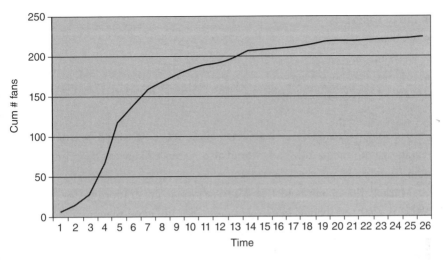

Figure 7.1: Rate of fans joining the Facebook fan page

of which is 217.5). For this particular campaign, we had no targets set for the number of fans, but if my client wanted at least 1,000 fans, we can see that at the point of critical mass, there is very little chance we could achieve that figure organically. However, if there were more fans at critical mass then obviously the final number of fans would also increase.

There are ways in which we could inflate the number of fans at critical mass by creating momentum for the page. This could take the form of advertising (whether through Facebook ads or other channels) or increasing the visibility of the page through cross promotion on other Facebook groups or traditional PR methods. By targeting relevant audiences, you are ensuring that the network effect remains – you are not targeting different, disparate groups of people, but you are targeting people likely to be linked within your target network. Homophily, the notion that "birds of a feather flock together", implies that people who have similar interests have a tendency to be part of the same network.

Alternatively, you could target those who have a vested interest in seeing your product or campaign succeed. Marketers trying to create a viral often immediately target the general public and the masses, forgetting that much of the time they have no interest in the content. Very simply, marketers could use internal resources such as owned communication channels including:

- Email databases
- Websites
- Newsletters
- Existing Facebook pages
- Related Facebook groups

These will already have established audiences who would be interested in engaging with the brand. They would also be more likely to share this content with friends and personal networks.

Mark Earls, in his book *Herd*, gives a great illustration of how this can work in a more practical sense. He describes his band playing a gig, saying that regardless of how good the band is "the trick to people really enjoying a gig [is to] get the audience interacting with each other . . . If you get enough people [dancing] early on, then their enjoyment seems to encourage the others, who in turn encourage others by example (rather than any obvious persuasion)." If Earls was struggling to get people to enjoy his band and he was desperate, he could potentially make sure his friends turn up to all his gigs and help kick start the dancing, encouraging others to join in.

SIR model and the spread of epidemics

William Kermack and A.G. McKendrick introduced the SIR model over 70 years ago to give some explanation for the spread of epidemics. The abbreviation, SIR, represents three states that a person can be in during the spread of a virus: susceptible, the person can still contract the virus but is not yet infected; infected, the person has the virus; and recovered, which could mean that the person is now removed from the equation either by recovering or dying. In Earls' scenario the susceptible would be those who are enjoying watching the other people dance and might get up later, the infected would be those that are already dancing and the recovered would be those who have finished dancing and/or gone home.

As well as creating momentum, marketers could also look at how they can make their content easier to spread in a network. Viruses, which are more contagious, or music, which appeals to a more mainstream audience, are more likely to spread. People are more likely to pass on good content (although obviously this is subjective). You could also help the viral spread by opening up new touch points (and therefore opportunities) for it to infect the susceptibles. Video sharing sites, social networks, emails and tweets could all provide opportunities to infect, and in just one click a person could spread the message to the whole of their social network with little to no cost to themselves.

Contagion is not persuasion

However, it's obviously not always so simple. Although viruses and trends can appear similar, influencing people's behaviour is slightly more complicated. There are a number of factors that influence whether a person adopts an innovation other than simply being exposed to it. These can be a combination of many things but generally fall into one of the following categories.

Informational – sometimes called "social recommendation", this can be in the form of simply taking advice from another person. The more you trust this person's knowledge in that particular area, the more influential this factor becomes.

Financial/mechanical – this refers to more functional or practical reasons for adopting an innovation and is related to Metcalfe's law where "the value of a telecommunications network is proportional to the square of the number of connected users of the system". For example, ten years ago businesses did not necessarily require emails to operate, but as more began using email systems, it put greater pressure on those not yet decided. Organizations that don't have email systems in place would find it difficult to communicate with many of their stakeholders.

Social – social pressure also plays a part during the adoption process. Peer pressure and the need to "fit in" with a certain group of people would be an example of social pressure. Wearing certain clothing and adjusting your opinion can help an individual to fit better into a group. Linked to this is also the idea of social currency, where people do certain things to help instigate communication and socialize. For example, when I was growing up, I remember the rich boy at school buying the latest video games just so he had a reason to ask people to go to his house. More recently, this idea of "social currency" could be seen in the number of people who went to watch the film *Avatar* just because they knew everyone else would be talking about it.

Lowering thresholds

Knowing which factors impact a person's decision can help businesses plan communications activities to effectively lower consumer thresholds and, thus, make it more likely that consumers will adopt an idea and, therefore, create enough momentum to help instigate a trend.

When people are weighing up whether to purchase a product there are several stages they go through. Firstly, during the early stage of purchase where the consumer is evaluating between different products on the market, there is an opportunity for brands to communicate examples of social recommendation. This is made easier for brands with the increasing number of channels the general public has at their disposal to communicate to their peers. A blogger outreach programme targeted at the relevant demographic would allow the consumer to see recommendations from similarly minded people. Making these visible – such as optimizing for search engines – would make them easier for the consumer to find.

In terms of lowering the mechanical threshold, a brand could increase the perception that more people have purchased the product by advertising or seeding stories in the media. For example, a large part of the reason why I purchased an XBOX 360 video games console over a PS3 was because more people I know already had one and so it made it much more useful for playing games online against friends. If more people are on XBOX's online portal, then it is more valuable to me. If it is perceived that more people have adopted a product, it also reduces the risk of purchase for the consumer – if people have already trialed the product then there is less chance of the product being faulty. (Let's ignore the whole Red Ring of Death fiasco.)

Related to this idea are what economists call *information cascades*. Information cascades occur when people observe what others are doing and follow their actions rather than relying on their own information and knowledge. An example of this would be eating out in a new city, where you would simply choose a place to dine based on how many people are also eating there at the time or in the case of Chinese restaurants, how many Chinese people specifically you can see eating there. (I'm of Chinese origin and it's strange that even I do this.)

The tactic of increasing visibility of a product can also reduce the social threshold for consumers. Branded clothing is an obvious example of how an endorsement by the latest actor or pop star can help create a trend. People see Jude Law in an advertisement wearing a cardigan and soon the pubs and clubs in UK towns become frequented by people in similar attire.

However, increased visibility and access can also have a reverse effect on adoption. If you happen to live in the Shoreditch area of East London, the more popular (i.e. mainstream) a product is, be it a band, item of clothing and so on, means that it loses its exclusivity and, therefore, much of its desirability with this demographic. Web companies often send out exclusive beta invites for the same reason – this scarcity increases the product's perceived value, which can then create discussions among consumers, fueling desire for the next round of beta invites.

Businesses could also consider generating momentum by targeting people who naturally have a lower threshold. This group of people, often called early adopters (Everett M. Rogers' *Diffusion of Innovations*, 1962), have more of a tendency to trial, adopt and discuss new products than other groups. Although it may be difficult to identify influencers, the web has made these early adopters more visible than in previous years.

Conclusion

With research into the role of influencers still relatively in its infancy, it is no surprise to find that not everyone is in agreement as to the effect it has on society. While the influentials theory remains endearing – and an easier sell to clients – there are a number of people who do not buy into it.

However, when we look at trends not just at the point where they suddenly breakout, but also at how and why they spread and the effect on people at a more granular level, a few aspects remain consistent (and are hardly mind blowing to most communications professionals).

Good content makes it more likely that people will pass on brand messaging. From the T-Mobile Liverpool Street flash mob, to the Compare the Meerkat ads, good content will be shared with friends. The advent of social media has made it even easier to do this.

Making as many people aware of the content as possible, whether it is through traditional or social media channels, means that more people will see it and, therefore, it is more likely to spread. As seen in Watts' research, theoretically anyone can start a trend: therefore, playing the numbers game to increase awareness also increases the likelihood that the content will trend. The media, whether through PR outreach or advertising, still remains a key channel for increasing awareness.

Lastly it is about context – knowing who your product is aimed at and how that person interacts with his or her peers. Although good content is subjective, making the content and the angle relevant for your target audience is not. If your product is targeted at a specific demographic, then creating content that appeals to them makes more sense than randomly targeting everyone. This is not about who is influential, but targeting people based on what they like will increase the chances that they pass on your content.

Roundup

Want more? See what has been said about this chapter or get involved and discuss it with the author and other readers on our LinkedIn group, find it by visiting http://www.socialmedia-mba.com or search for "The Social Media MBA Alumni".

Social media has bridged the gap between media and interpersonal influence. While everyone has the potential to be influential, conversely it means that those who were perceived to be more influential are less so. Businesses should not only focus on targeting the cool, influential kids, but understand how messages spread through different networks and perhaps look at reaching out to the people who actually buy the products, i.e. Average Joe.

A way to increase the number of opportunities you have to connect with a greater range of people is to take a "bottom-up" or "grass root" approach, encourage your staff to share their expertise or connect with customers. This will be discussed in the next chapter by Euan Semple.

References

Rogers, Everett M. (1962) *Diffusion of Innovations*. Simon & Schuster International; 5th Revised edition edition (17 Nov 2003).

Two Step Flow Theory (2004) Opleidingswebsite Communicatiewetenschap (CW) En Communication Studies (CS). University of Twente, 9 September, 2004. Web 11 Apr. 2010.

Part III

Strategy Delivery

Chapter 8

Helping staff share expertise with customers is the best way to build your brand

Euan Semple

In short

- How conversations are marketing.
- Why staff network matters.
- What customers want from you in social media.

Overview

In this chapter Euan Semple, who has worked on social media projects for organizations like the BBC, World Bank and Nato, explains why conventional advertising and marketing have had their day. Being "targeted" and having "campaigns" aimed at you feels more like combat than custom.

People are suspicious of the artifice of television advertising, preferring the viral video or genius tweet to the expensive ad or press release driven copy. Given these shifting expectations I will make the case in this chapter that your staff have the potential to be your best advocates and customers will increasingly want real conversations with real people working in the companies whose products they buy. Cut the cost of your expensive ad agencies and start having your own conversations with your own customers in a tone that suits them and in the places they want to meet you. The chapter will explore the whys and hows of staff advocacy and lay out the risks and benefits to your business of adopting this radical way of reconnecting with both your customers and your staff.

Marketing

Brand used to mean the trust resulting from consistently high quality products or behaviour. Increasingly it means carefully managed spin. In addition, most marketing feels like being shouted at when you are trying to do something else. Seth Godin describes it as interruptive rather than permissive. Whether it is TV ads or hoardings on the street, businesses attempt to grab our attention while we are trying to do something else. Online banner ads and pop-ups on the web work on the same principle and most of us end up finding ways to block them.

Along comes social media and the next thing you know millions of people are having online conversations about everything under the sun – including the products they aspire to or have bought. Cue a rush of marketing departments, assisted by agencies, clamouring to become our "friends" online and to intrude on our conversations with yet more of the same interruptive thinking that they have been peddling for years! What we end up with is the 140 character press release. The same shouty content delivered in a new form on Twitter. People aren't even liking companies' Facebook pages – literally. Very few of them are pressing the like button in response to marketing campaigns. Trying to import old ways of connecting with customers into the new environments isn't working.

It is ten years ago that Doc Searls put his finger on the potential of the web for the marketing industry with his now famous phrase "markets are conversations" and these conversations are increasingly taking place online. The kinds of connections that are fostered by conversations are very powerful, in fact the ones that we have been shown to trust the most. In the past these conversations have been lost around the water cooler – now you can get to see them. The raving fan of your products is visible to you, you can see what he or she is saying and you can reach out to connect with them.

What if by allowing more direct contact between your staff and your customers you were able to get back to the original meaning of brand? Back to real conversations with real people about real products and building your brand one conversation at a time? Here is a way to connect staff with customers and, scary though that might seem, it is the most powerful opportunity to have conversations and build relationships with your clients in a way which has never been possible before.

Conversations

So what is this elusive thing called a conversation that businesses and marketing people seem to find so difficult to "get". In the early days of blogging there was a lot of talk about "finding your voice" and "authenticity". The third person, corporate voice jars in this interpersonal world of social media. Finding an appropriate tone is one of the things organizations find hardest about talking on the web and the professional business communicator has forgotten how to talk normally! Those used to the more constrained world of business communication find it difficult to use a more direct and conversational tone. "Corporations don't tweet – people do."

Conversations are two way. As David Weinberger author of *The Cluetrain Manifesto* said, "Conversations can only take place between equals." In other words if it is going to be a conversation rather than a pitch or a lecture both participants have to be on an equal footing with mutual tolerance and respect. This is hard when one of them is an institution.

Much of what works on the social web relies on reciprocity – the willingness to do something in return for having been helped in some way – and reciprocity relies on mutual respect. When you are treating me as a statistic, or worse a target, I don't feel respected and have little inclination to reciprocate. Why should I retweet your tweets or like your Facebook page when you won't even tell me your name?

Once you learn how to, even statements can be written in such a way as to invite ongoing conversation in contrast to the "talk to the hand" tone of much conventional writing. The trouble is that trying too hard can result in looking like your Dad dancing at a disco. You are proud of him for having a go but really rather wish he wasn't! This issue of conversations is still a big challenge to many unfamiliar with writing for the web and is one of the reasons that it is easier for ordinary staff than it is for professionals.

Staff networks

So, given that conventional marketing isn't as effective as it used to be, and professional communicators find it hard to get the tone of conversations right, what should you do? Well, you already have hundreds if not thousands of people who work for you taking part on a daily basis in conversations with all sorts of interesting and possibly influential people on the web. Why not enlist their support, tap into their networks, and get some real conversations going between real people about real products?

Your staff will be booking holidays and buying products online. Increasingly the sites that provide those services include a social platform of some sort. Product pages sit alongside personal profiles in Facebook and the demarcation between work and home is getting much less clear. Given that your staff is spending time in these spaces and the chances of your business coming up in conversation are increasing, why not pre-empt the situation and make the most of it instead of dreading it.

> Knowing who you are connected to and how you rate them has always counted for more than taking a blind chance in Yellow Pages or your corporate directory.

Work has always consisted of networks. Networks are how we pass on information and how we confer trust and respect. Knowing who you are connected to and how you rate them has always counted for more than taking a blind chance in Yellow Pages or your corporate directory. Working out who is the best person to talk to or ask for help from is best done through networks. All the web does is to extend your network beyond face to face and beyond the constraints of the physical world.

The kinds of connections possible through your staff's own online networks are going to be so much more authentic than anything that has been possible before. Fostering these kind of networks brings with it an obligation and responsibility that isn't easy but can be so powerful. Allowing customers to see more of how you do what you do may seem intimidating at first but increasingly customers want to have an insight into what you do, and why, for all sorts of reasons, some good and some bad. You obviously have to manage how much you make open but anything is better than the high blank wall of professional communications they face now. People are fascinated by the real even if that can sometimes feel ordinary. Rob Paterson refers to this as "the intensity of the mundane". It is a million miles away from the glamour or shock of the new and exciting that dominates conventional marketing. It is nerdy, it is focussed enthusiasm, attention to detail, intimate interest.

Culture

Your corporate culture will be a significant factor in your ability to tap into staff advocacy. There is little point aspiring to be 2.0 outside the firewall when you can't even manage to be 1.0 inside. You will simply not have the competence to undertake online relationships and if your internal communication channels are archaic then you won't have the speed or agility to respond appropriately to what is happening in the much faster moving online world. If you have an overly rigid command and control culture then the unpredictability of this networked world is going to feel alien and challenging for many of your managers. Also if staff members are used to waiting to be told what to do and are not used to thinking for themselves then speaking up online about what they do is going to be a real stretch for them.

Many organizations and managers fear loss of control if they give staff access to these tools. Well, the bad news is you never really had control. You may have had the appearance of control but people could always say what they wanted around the water cooler or in the pub after work. At least with online tools you get to see what they are saying and use the tools to respond. If you get good at using online tools you can vastly increase your influence and thereby your ability to "control" what is being said about you by both staff and customers. Indeed your managers are part of your staff and are in many ways the very ones you want to be connected with the outside world. If your managers get good at blogging internally, which you should seriously consider, and become insightful of the interesting twists and turns of your business why not let some of their insights be seen by the outside world. There are many businesses I buy from where I would love to know more about the hows and whys of their business.

You will have to have confidence not only in your staff but also in your product or service. If you don't then you are increasingly going to have a problem anyway. As Dave Winer says, "If you don't want me to slag off your product on the internet don't have a shit product": and this is the rather uncomfortable bottom line we all inevitably reach. This will be true for your staff too. If they are at all uncomfortable about what you do or your products they are going to be reticent about singing your praises online. If your members of staff are going to represent you in their online lives then they will have to feel confident enough to do so. They will have to have confidence in themselves and their opinions but also in your work and your support of them. You are going to have to face these issues some time.

I was with Vint Cerf, one of the inventors of the internet, when he was asked by a journalist whether he thought, looking back over the last 30 years, that the internet was a good or bad thing. His response was "It is just a thing. Whether you see it as good or bad depends what you are doing with it and that is a reflection of what you are as an individual, an organization, or a society and if you don't like what you are doing then that is what you have to fix." This is true of you too. If you, or your staff, don't like what is being said about you on the internet or don't feel happy about some of the things you are doing then that is what you have to be worried about – not the internet.

Competence

So if your staff are your best hope for authentic conversations with customers and your management culture is up for letting them do so, what do you need to do to make it work?

Deciding who should be representing you online can be problematic. The temptation is to decide by job function or role. The problem is that there is no guarantee that the people in those positions "get" the web or are already active online. You will have to compromise and go with those who have experience and existing networks. Be very sensitive about how you approach them though, they will understandably be wary of the misuse of their influence and will need to feel comfortable about your motives. This may well be the single biggest hurdle you face – how do you throw back, in some cases, years of conditioning and encourage staff to trust you enough to take responsibility for speaking on your behalf. If you get it right they will not only be willing to access their own network but may also be willing to ask their network to reach out to their own networks, thereby opening up potentially huge numbers of people. This will only happen though if they all feel comfortable with what is being asked of them.

When things go wrong

Inevitably you will get things wrong and annoy your customers. In fact being criticized on the internet is one of the great fears of corporations and makes them wary of engaging in online dialogue with their customers. But you are being discussed online whether you like it or not and when things do go wrong it is better to be aware of the conversations and be in a position to take part in them than it is to hide and pretend they are not happening. If your staff have existing and positive online relations with customers then when the shit does hit the fan you have a group of people at least willing to listen to your perspective and, if you do a good enough job, who will spread your version of events for you amongst their own networks.

Speed matters online. News, and gossip, can spread faster than ever before. Having your staff already engaged in online conversations about your business means that a) you get to know faster if something is going wrong and b) you are able to do something about it before it escalates into something worse. There have been many examples recently where corporations have not only been unaware of problems brewing online but have done too little too late and often the wrong thing! This can be avoided if you help your staff to help you.

Some of those already engaged online can feel swamped. If you are the only communications person in a large organization charged with managing their online conversations it can quickly become too much to handle and you can feel as if you have to have three sets of eyes and ears and never sleep. Why not spread the load amongst your fellow staff? Why not access the support of people who are online anyway and help them to help you? Apart from anything else you won't know the answers to all of the questions that come up so why not pass the burden on to those that do?

Increasingly the press are picking up on what is being talked about in social media tools. Whether it is national disasters or your latest packaging, someone somewhere online is breaking the news and journalists are picking up on these sources to find the stories that hit the headlines. The sheer speed and directness of these sources trumps press releases every time and if you were to allow your staff to talk online about what they do they could get you ahead of the competition in terms of fast, effective communication with the press for virtually no cost.

Benefits

So we have looked at the problems with marketing, decided to let your staff become your online advocates, had a look at how you might go about making this work and even considered some of the risks. What, in addition to increased influence, do you get for all of your efforts?

Being part of direct conversations with your customers gives you the best market qualitative insights you are likely to get. Yes you will want to continue with surveys and other more quantifiable measures of your success, but having an ongoing relationship with the people buying your product or service has never been so easy. Especially if these conversations are with your own staff, then everyone has an ongoing and a current appreciation of your market and your position in it.

Instead of making decisions in the dark you will have a greater confidence about what you are doing and why. You won't be acting in isolation but with the involvement of whole communities. This will be true at both the strategic and operational levels. Everyone will know so much more about the context for their decisions that those decisions will inevitably improve. You will also be seen as a company confident enough in your product or service to engage with real customers rather than one maintaining a safe distance.

Imagine staff at all levels being in a position to engage in conversations about new products and new directions. Instead of putting all of your faith in marketing and R&D you can have a much wider pool of opportunity. It doesn't mean you have to respond to every daft idea but you can widen your range of possibilities at little or no cost. Innovation is one of the things that all businesses see as essential but they will tend to set up a committee to handle it while at the same time customers are screaming out solutions and opportunities online.

Increasingly those who have grown up with the web will make decisions about who they want to work with on the basis of how network friendly their prospective employers are. If your staff is already active online, and extolling the virtues of working for you, this is the most robust way to engage your future stars.

Once your members of staff have moved on, either into retirement or even to other employers, there is a strong chance they will want to maintain links with people still in your organization. They will do this anyway through LinkedIn or Facebook but why not encourage them to become an active part of your alumni and continue to contribute even in some small way to your ongoing success?

By engaging now in these platforms and allowing your staff to become your advocates you are going to be well ahead of the competition and be building networks and behaviours that will inevitably become more widespread. Future proof your organization and your staff by building competence and networks sooner rather than later.

Roundup

> Want more? See what has been said about this chapter or get involved and discuss it with the author and other readers on our LinkedIn group, find it by visiting http://www.socialmedia-mba.com or search for "The Social Media MBA Alumni".

There is little doubt that more of our lives will be spent connected online through a whole range of devices in such a way that almost everything we do will be touched by it. We are still in a position where many are not sure of or haven't had much experience online and businesses still hold it at arm's length. To generations who are growing up with the web this is not the same and for them it is just one of the places where they conduct their lives. In fact what we are talking about here is not making something happen but in many cases trying to stop something that is trying to happen anyway. All you have to do at one level is stop stopping it happening!

Your staff use social tools anyway, and they are going to talk about what you do anyway, so why not make this an opportunity rather than a threat? Great rewards are available to those who truly adopt the idea that "markets are conversations" and companies who trust their employees enough to let them become their best advocates will attract the brightest and most motivated staff.

Given the inevitability of this – why not get started today? Find that member of staff who is defending your honour in that Facebook discussion. Watch them, learn from them, make friends with them and enlist their help. Who knows, you might start joining in the conversation.

Trying new things is vital but the ROI should always be considered. In the next chapter David Marrinan-Hayes identifies ten key points to remember when planning a social media activity.

Chapter 9

Ten rules to ensure positive ROI on your social media activity

David Marrinan-Hayes

In short

- Why the biggest roadblocks to successful social media ROI come from within organizations not from consumers.
- How badly implemented social media will deliver negative ROI.
- What those who generate the biggest ROI do so well.

Overview

In this chapter David Marrinan-Hayes, Commercial Director at British media company Archant (http://www.archant.co.uk/), discusses the social media return on investment. How much should you be spending on social media depends on your goals. Utilizing social media in certain areas – journalism, customer services, product development – can substantially cut costs and be far more effective at managing your customer image. The chapter discusses ten important aspects to consider, with good and bad examples of well-known brands and their social media campaigns.

Picture this: the links back to YouTube spread like wildfire. Across Twitter, Facebook and email hashtags, wall posts and links were propagating and re-propagating. Tech and media bloggers, the mainstream press and the broadcast networks were all picking up the story, driving interest even higher. Within the first 24 hours 5.9 million people had viewed the videos: more than had watched Obama's inauguration speech; more than had watched George Bush dodge a flying shoe; more even than had watched Susan Boyle's audition. What was fuelling the frenzy? A newly released celebrity sex tape? A political expose of Watergate proportions? Actually, it was a series of videos for that most unfashionable of men's grooming products, Old Spice, the preserve of aging playboys and high school geography teachers. Except now it wasn't: some of the world's leading influencers were not only talking about the brand, they were actively engaging with it.

It was a spectacular success. Sales of the brand rose 25 per cent after the campaign was executed and Old Spice was no longer the nerdiest kid on the block.

So what had Old Spice done to beat some of the market-leading brands in driving mind-share and, more importantly, market share to deliver back a spectacular return on investment (ROI)?

The cynical, sore losers and poorly performing incumbents (who are often one and the same) tend to write all these social media successes off as luck – serendipitous quirks that cannot be repeated and are not relevant to their businesses in any case.

Delve deeper and the real answer was that Old Spice tapped into a large proportion of the underlying emotional factors that drive people to engage with – and more importantly positively share – brand experiences via key social media channels. In this instance the factors were relevance, joy and originality. In addition, Old Spice displayed a brace of the organizational factors that can harness these emotions into a coherent consumer proposition; in short the campaign was creatively disruptive, unique, suited the medium, was well resourced and rewarded consumers for their input.

What is return on investment?

The answer used to be simple, profit generated from investment/cost of investment, but social media is so broad that it means very different things depending on your place in the social media ecosystem. In fact the whole concept of whether ROI is relevant is subject to fierce debate when it comes to the use of social media channels.

Are you looking to effect social change? Are you looking to open up new channels of communication or optimize operations for an existing organization? Or are you launching a new product or service that has social media at its core? Social media can positively impact them all but, for the purposes of this chapter, we are focusing on looking at ROI when using social media for marketing and communications.

Let's begin with a note of caution. As we've already seen, the realm of social media is moving fast. Not Usain Bolt fast: meteor fast. Social media product popularity shifts on a dime. There was a time when the world's biggest brands were embracing Second Life and MySpace. Now it's Facebook, Twitter and Foursquare. Social media marketing practices that were cutting edge and driving millions of dollars in revenue 12 months ago are now either so pervasive as to be ineffectual or no longer permissible.

The point being, social media strategy comes with a large portion of planned obsolescence so it's a fair bet that a number of the case studies and tactics discussed in this chapter will be old news by the time you read them. But the underlying principles remain the same; so as long as you apply the principles and not necessarily the practices you'll be well on the way to a black-ink situation.

Here is a ten point check list to understand your ROI

1. Know thyself – a little introspection can save a lot of money

It's not an unfamiliar story. The call comes from the CEO's office. He wants the company on Twitter. Where is the company's social media strategy? He wants to go big – all social all the time. He wants it by Friday. Plans are drawn up, budgets are composed and PowerPoints are written. The presentation is made; the company is going to engage in a genuine two-way conversation with its customers to build a better business. Brows are furrowed. Words like "genuine" and "two-way" are repeated warily and then it comes: the pronouncement.

He really just wants the PR team to use it to link to press releases. Social media should be used to convey good news. Customer service should be left to the call centres. You give the Twitter account to the intern to run, or worse the CEO, and three weeks later you have a PR nightmare on your hands.

The surest way to create negative value for your organization is to rush headlong into any strategy without proper planning, support or buy-in. Ask Habitat, Vodafone, Kenneth Cole, Nestle or Chrysler. Study after study shows that bad strategy well executed is better than good strategy badly executed.

Sadly, for reasons of leadership, culture and operational infrastructure, most businesses' social media strategies fall into the latter category. From blue chip down to Mom-and-Pop, businesses are blowing their social media strategy by not executing properly.

As touched on in previous chapters, social media is too important to be left to any one department to own outright. If you think it can then you have already failed. Those companies who succeed in the social media realm are those who believe in and embrace the opportunity it presents. Before one dollar is spent on social media it is worth taking a look at the DNA of our business to understand the likelihood that it has what it takes to succeed.

> Before one dollar is spent on social media it is worth taking a look at the DNA of our business to understand the likelihood that it has what it takes to succeed.

These are not easy questions to answer – much less to ask if you are not the CEO and have been given ownership of social media strategy. These are not tactical type questions that are going into developing a business plan but are the kind of philosophical questions the whole organization needs to consider. Such as:

- Why are we doing this?
- Are we box-ticking to please investors or directors?
- Do we understand what social media is?
- Do we think social media is relevant to our business?
- Does our business already have problems with basic digital change?
- Do we have the desire to make social media successful no matter what the challenges?

Honest answers are vital. The truth is, the biggest roadblocks to social media success will come from within your own organization. Unlike marketing and communications channels of old you will not be in control of this one. Whether you like it or not consumers already have an implicit understanding of what they want to get from you via social media channels and if you don't meet those criteria you've already failed and blown your chances of delivering successful ROI.

2. Motives and means – understanding the inputs and outputs

Once you have answered to your satisfaction the macro questions about your company's strategic need for social media investment it's time to take a more tactical view. For most organizations it's probably too late for this piece of advice, but before any social media activity is commenced it's worth understanding what your objectives and key performance indicators (KPIs) are.

Most companies launch headfirst into the world of social media with the most basic of strategic intents where the setting up of a Facebook page, a Twitter account or a YouTube channel becomes an end in itself rather than a means to an end. Either that or a tactic – such as a product launch or competition idea – drives the strategy, rather than the other way round.

Either way, launching into the world of 24/7 communications with consumers without clear company-wide objectives is failing before you have even begun.

Can you say with certainty that even the most basic of strategies are understood within your organization? Could any employee in your company, if asked, answer in ten words or less what the purpose of each of these outlets is? Could you, if pushed, come up with a stand-alone P&L for your social media activity that offset the value of consumer acquisition and retention against the costs of maintaining these channels on a permanent basis?

Delivering successful ROI is based on first knowing what your R is:

- Are you looking to reduce operations costs?
- Are you looking for cheaper user acquisition channels?
- Are you looking to improve customer service?
- Are you trying to launch new products?

And then figuring out the appropriate I:

- What is the capital investment required?
- What is the human resource required?
- What are the timeframes for delivery?

Once you understand the R and the I you can focus on joining them with the O.

3. Will it play in Peoria? – or why relevance = revenues

Put your hands up if you remember Second Life. Now, hands up if you not only remember Second Life but invested six figures plus plenty of hyperbole in putting your brand into the virtual realm.

Don't worry you're not alone. At the peak of Second Life mania, in the second half of 2006, businesses from *Fortune* 500 companies to local crafters were setting up shop there and the media couldn't report it fast enough.

Adidas created digital trainers, *The Guardian* sponsored a film festival, Toyota set up a car dealership and Reuters and Sky both opened dedicated news bureaus. The press loved it. The problem was that customers didn't. They built it but nobody came. Budgets dried up, campaigns were quietly shelved and branded islands disappeared into the sea.

The conversation stopped. The problem was brands had gotten so wrapped up in the hype around the medium that they didn't stop to understand the message they were trying to convey and who would actually see it. In the rush not to be left out, brands never stopped to ask if they should have even been in. The pursuit of PR became a strategy in itself. Unless it's April Fools' Day no product should ever be launched with the sole intention of generating press attention.

Before you allocate marketing budget to any social media activity you need to ask yourself some fairly basic questions. Does the medium match your brand? Do its users? Will the cost of development match value of the campaign? Who am I doing this for – my consumers or my press cuttings file?

Not every social media channel will suit every business. B2B won't thrive on Facebook; FMCGs are best suited for Four Square. Whilst there may be pressure to be everywhere it's better to have several well-supported campaigns on relevant mediums than non-supported channels across the web.

4. Manning the gates – forget the intern, empower your staff

There are two ways you can experience failure of communications via social media. The first are the tweets heard around the world. By and large they are the tweets or status updates sent out by under-supervised interns and CEOs who don't have the experience to "check before they wreck".

Two classic examples from come Kenneth Cole and Habitat:

> "Millions are in uproar in #Cairo," the tweet read. "Rumor is they heard our new spring collection is now available online at http://bit.ly/KCairo-KC."

> "#Mousavi Join the database for free and win £1000 gift card http://bit.ly/2wPLO. Now!!"

One from a CEO, one from an intern; both calamitous failures but, despite the embarrassment these types of errors cause, they are easy to fix. It's clear they are wrong and a rapid and strongly-worded apology usually closes the issue down.

The second type is by far the more insidious of the two. It's the "we care but we don't" use of social media as a customer service channel. It's the more dangerous because it engenders long-term, slow burning negativity towards your brand: it uses social media for the exact opposite of what it's intended for – to be a direct, real-time open channel of communication.

As previously mentioned customers have a strong expectation of what they want from brands and if your brand has a social media presence and they make a complaint what they want is a resolution. Now. They don't want your intern to tweet an apology and direct them to a toll-free customer service number where they have to deal with some one-on-one who is reading from a script. That's why they complained in public in the first place.

If you are going to invest in social media channels you need to be realistic about the fact that customers will use them as their primary channels of complaint. Freeing your social media team to deal with them as consumers expect will increase goodwill, loyalty and positive word of mouth and ROI.

5. Be your own worst enemy – embracing disruption as a strategy

Innovation comes from disruption and profit comes from innovation. Nowhere is this more true than online in general and via social media in particular. The opportunity for cost reduction, reach expansion, revenue generation and customer acquisition is huge. It's also measureable, flexible and has a lower overhead on your business, and very often the environment, than the alternatives.

Take customer communication. Does your company publish a glossy monthly magazine, which it sends out to all its customers extolling successes, pushing new products, encouraging engagement, maintaining brand awareness? How much does it cost? How many people read it? Does it achieve its objectives? A well-run Facebook page can achieve all that a 60-page monthly magazine can do for a fraction of the cost if there is the will and desire to do so. Even better, that same well-run Facebook page can also act as a driver of new customers.

Every month in the UK *Sky Magazine* is sent, at considerable cost, to over 7 million UK homes. There's journalism, production, printing, postage and packaging to pay for. Every one print adds incremental costs. No one has asked for it – it is a push commutations tool.

Now take Starbucks – they have 25 million Facebook fans. The Starbucks Frappacino page on Facebook has 7 million fans of its own. There is no way logistically or financially Starbucks would have the communications infrastructure to communicate with these fans via any other medium. Embracing Facebook has given Starbucks a direct communications channel with 25 million people who have actively associated themselves with their brand.

Throughout every business there are opportunities to use social media to disrupt existing, expensive practices. You just need to identify them. Using your strategic intent and performance metrics as a guide, look and see what you could be doing cheaper via social media. Look inwards to see which existing practices and procedures you could change. Is it saving on postage for letters? Is it forgoing print advertising for direct communication with consumers? Is it using social media infrastructure and audience to launch your business into new territories as opposed to opening up new offices?

The most successful companies will not try to apply a one size fits all approach to social media. Those that thrive will be the ones that look at each department within the organization and understand how social media can help improve operations and income. The key will be ensuring they are working harmoniously, which is material for another chapter.

6. Right hand meet left hand – good communications leads to good campaigns

In July 2011 the world learnt of the launch of MoviePass, a new mobile and social media driven service that would allow consumers to buy all-you-can-eat cinema attendance in cinemas across the US for $50 a month. Consumers were thrilled. The movie industry was about to be disrupted in the consumers' favour. Business would boom and cinema attendance would soar. There was only one problem. No one bothered to ask the movie chains if they wanted to be disrupted. They didn't. Within two days the much-vaunted beta trial was dead in the water and at the time of writing the fate of the business hung in the balance.

This is an extreme example but it illustrates the importance of good communication when delivering social media campaigns. Internally PR might be run by the communications team, marketing by the marketing team, customer services by the customer service team and digital strategy by the digital team – all with different Vice Presidents and objectives. Except online that doesn't work. Consumers don't care about the internal dynamics of your organization, they care about hearing from you when you've got good things to say and getting help when they have bad things to say.

Like the cinema chains, if you are about to embark on a social media activity that is going to have an impact on another department then make sure they know about it. All your creative ideas and marketing spend will come to nothing if your customer services team feel left out in the cold and refuse to help customers when they call.

Likewise, if multiple areas of your business are engaging separately with consumers via social media channels, ensure there is enough co-ordination so as to make the consumers' life easier not more difficult. No consumer wants to be told that they need to talk to a different department. Not on the phone and definitely not online. Good communications will prevent the not-invented-here problem of a lack of ownership and ensure that all departments are primed to serve your customers as they want to be served. And a happy customer is a repeat customer and a brand advocate.

7. Joy to the world – why making it Christmas every day will turn your customers into advocates and deliver sales

There is a reason people look forward to Christmas. It's not just the presents and it's seldom the thought of three days cooped up with the in-laws. It's primarily subconscious but it's because, for the six weeks leading up to the holidays every year, the advertising and media industries, whose stock-in-trade for most of the year is fear, insecurity and most of the seven deadly sins, pedal a different emotion: joy.

It may be schmaltzy, saccharine and cynical, but it resonates. The emotions trickle down from marketing messages to the real world. In a high-pressure, eat-or-be-eaten world, for a few weeks each December businesses and consumers all go that extra mile to deliver better service and be nicer to one another. Everyone has a story of the airline that moved heaven and earth to get someone home; the delivery guy who ensured the presents were delivered despite a snow drift; the cashiers who smile and the customers who tip better.

The irony of all of this is that it very seldom costs any extra to bring joy to consumers' lives; it just takes a change of mindset. Positive messages cost the same to broadcast as passive-aggressive ones, employees cost the same whether they are smiling or scowling. Refunding an unhappy current customer is generally cheaper than finding a new one.

In the realms of the social media world this is even more true. In a world where 71 per cent of consumers will now research a business or a brand before purchasing, your reputation is your calling card. Amplification of communication means your customers can either become your worst enemies or your best advocates. On social media the dialogue is open for all to see. A bad reputation online costs far more to clean up than preventing it in the first place.

A key tenet of every social media campaign should be to elicit joy from your consumers and to empower those delivering your message to engender it. Committing to deliver a good customer service will always pay back in the long run.

8. There can be only one original – the importance of being unique in delivering viral social media campaigns

There are some things that all businesses should do consistently via social media channels. Call it the customer care charter: they should maintain those channels as much as if not more than any other; they should respond to customers openly and in real time; and they should ensure that all communication is seamless, honest and respectful. These are the foundations of driving successful long-term customer relationships.

There is a whole other use of social media, customer recruitment and brand awareness where consistency with the competition is not only not good, it's positively lazy, and almost guaranteed to deliver a poor ROI. This strand of activity we generally shorthand with the "V" word: viral.

Well executed viral marketing can achieve stunning ROI for businesses. As we've seen from the Old Spice campaign it can not only drive sales but also reposition your entire brand. Unfortunately, like their microbial namesakes, good viral campaigns require a healthy combination of criteria to be successful, the most important of which is uniqueness.

It's the easiest thing in the world to look at a competitor's viral activity and try a variation on the same theme; but to understand successful viral activity is to need to understand the reasons for something going viral in the first place.

The *New Yorker* hid an article by Jonathan Franzen about David Foster Wallace behind a Facebook-like wall and asked people to friend them to see if they generated 17,000 new fans in a week. Not only did the articles generate a huge new audience for the magazine to market to but they also drove considerable PR for the campaign itself. It worked not only because it was a fresh idea but also because the value of the reward was equal to the effort of liking the page in the first place.

The activity inspired a huge number of imitators who didn't do nearly as well because marketers made the mistake of assuming consumers would expend effort for any old reward. They won't. Consumers will reward innovation and uniqueness. Before being inspired by a campaign you've seen elsewhere ask yourself whether consumers are likely to feel the same way.

9. Look before you leap – understand the medium before you convey the message

What you think will work well on a given medium and what your consumers think are two very different things. Like the CEO who only wants to use social media channels to push good news and thinks this will suffice, the assumption that consumers will consume any old data just because it's coming from your brand is false.

Before launching onto any social media platform it's important that the first thing you properly evaluate is what information consumers want to receive, not what information you want to share.

This information is often not what you'd think. When newspapers first launched onto Twitter the assumption was that consumers would follow newspapers to get a feed of shortened headlines that would drive traffic through to newspaper websites. As it transpired users do not want feeds full of endless links. It was a lazy use of Twitter and an example of where businesses put their own objectives – driving traffic – above the needs of the consumer – getting real time information. Things changed dramatically when journalists started using Twitter as a medium for breaking the news itself, rather than merely delivering out of date headlines. The message was changed to suit the medium and everyone benefited.

When evaluating your communications strategy put yourself in the consumer's shoes. Understand what they want to hear from you about. Hell – ask them; then ensure you deliver it. In a world where the cost of set-up and delivery is the same no matter what the size of your business, if you don't give your consumers what they want chances are someone else will. This will not only affect your ROI – it will have a long-term impact on the survival of your business.

10. Now what? – a customer is for life not just a campaign

Life was simple in the past. You had a new product that you wanted people to experience so you set up a sampling campaign or promotional drive. Lots of fresh-faced young things would hand out your product at train stations, department stores and festivals or a TV ad would exhort the customer to call for a free sample pack. The product would either be delivered with a smile or a nice marketing letter. The customer tried it and if they liked it they converted. The pact was explicit. We give, you take. If you like it you'll buy some more.

This is not the case today. Whilst the fresh-faced young things are probably still part of the mix – TV ads exhort customers to like your Facebook page instead of making a call to collect a free sample. The product is delivered with a nice marketing letter and so the pack goes. Except this time it's different. It's not a campaign any more; it's a party. In the past the communication would be finite, now you have hundreds if not thousands of people with a permanent connection to your brand. You'd never invite consumers to an event or research panel and assume that getting them into the building was your job done and go home. You'd wine and dine them. You'd listen to what they have to say. You'd thank them for coming and reward their loyalty. You'd probably follow-up with a thank you. And so it goes with social media.

You may still only want to run a campaign but once it's done you have to clean up. Nothing communicates bad customer services like a page that hasn't been updated in months. People who find it won't know it's a campaign and will just assume you don't care.

When drawing up a fixed-term social media marketing campaign consider the exit strategy. What do you want to do with these customers once your competition or sampling campaign or special offer expires? Should you migrate them to another page? Should you post a clear message thanking everybody for their participation and recommending they engage with you more permanently elsewhere? Can you keep the campaign page updated after the campaign has finished? You have gone to a lot of time and trouble to generate new customers for your business and some simple pre-planning can save a lot of long-term negative perception and even realize greater value from consumers long after their original value was realized.

Roundup

Want more? See what has been said about this chapter or get involved and discuss it with the author and other readers on our LinkedIn group. Find it by visiting http://www.socialmedia-mba.com or search for "The Social Media MBA Alumni".

Some people get offended when you ask them to explain the ROI of a social media campaign; is this because they don't know what it means, why it is important or how to measure it?

If we want the support of our leadership team to continue to invest in social media, being able to break down our project proposals or results from previous projects to an ROI is a powerful tool for gaining their trust and support.

But we also have to be honest with ourselves. David asks, is your company a box ticker or a box buster? Does it have the DNA to properly take advantage of the opportunities presented by social media? What about you? Have you got the necessary diplomacy, guerrilla and innovation skills to constantly adapt?

In the next chapter Jed Hallam will develop the idea of social media creating value for the business beyond social media vanity.

Chapter 10

Using social technology to augment business strategy and achieve real business objectives

Jed Hallam

In short

- How social media has developed beyond marketing.
- Why social technology plays a significant role in the consumer journey.
- How to develop a social business strategy.

Overview

In this chapter Jed Hallam, Communities Director at VCCP where he develops social strategies for clients such as O2, MORE TH>N and Unilever, discusses the life cycle of the social media industry and explains how innovation will help you to improve your business strategy and produce bottom-line impact through social media and digital technology.

As a precursor to what I'm about to say, the models and suggestions I'm putting forward are either existing and established ideas or are concepts that I have worked on with live clients. However, please remember that this industry is still relatively new and that these concepts are iterative models that are developing every day.

Social media industry life cycle

For me, one of the most interesting things about any technology or business is how it evolves, which has been particularly useful as my job has always been focused on innovation and strategy. About 18 months ago, a friend of mine (Tim Hoang, who you'll find in this book too) spoke to me about Everett Rogers' *Diffusion of Innovations* (1962). At the time we were discussing how we could track the way in which messages moved from one person to another and trying to mastermind network mechanics. I then started reading a little more widely on adoption and development theories and became increasingly interested in life cycles.

These theories can help us to predict which services, products, agencies and industries are going to be important in the future – which is incredibly valuable in such a fast moving industry.

This led me to begin plotting my own work (developing products and services) against Theodore Levitt's theory of product life cycles (PLCs) (1965) and trying to figure out at which point I'd oversaturated our clients and needed to look at reinvigorating things.

One evening I was reading about different aspects of how the PLC model had been used by different industries over the past 50 years and I found Steven Klepper's work on industry life cycles (ILCs) (1997). Things began to click a little more with how I could apply these models to social media (services, agencies and the industry) and use the models to think smarter about how social media would develop as whole.

Figure 10.1 shows Klepper's ILC, it's a simple graph that highlights the four key areas of an industry's development; birth, growth, maturity and decline.

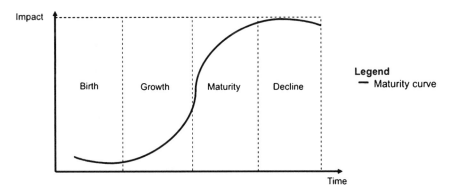

Figure 10.1: Industry life cycle analysis

Klepper probably explains the phases better than I could:

Three stages of evolution are distinguished. In the initial, exploratory or embryonic stage, market volume is low, uncertainty is high, the product design is primitive, and unspecialized machinery is used to manufacture the product. Many firms enter and competition based on product innovation is intense.

In the second, intermediate or growth stage, output growth is high, the design of the product begins to stabilize, product innovation declines, and the production process becomes more refined as specialized machinery is substituted for labor. Entry slows and a shakeout of producers occurs.

Stage three, the mature stage, corresponds to a mature market. Output growth slows, entry declines further, market share stabilizes, innovations are less significant, and management, marketing and manufacturing techniques become more refined.

The notion of applying this ILC to the social media industry is a little bit on the lightweight side until you overlay the ILC analysis with Everett's adoption curve and begin to plot out where certain brands fit within the analysis.

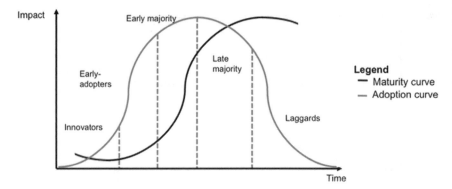

Figure 10.2: Industry life cycle and adoption analysis

It's even possible to begin matching dates to the x-axis – the "innovators" period could quite comfortably be around 2000/2001 and it's fair to say that we're currently (in 2011) experiencing the late majority/laggards phase. This would suggest that the industry is maturing and we're (potentially) about to hit a period Hugo Hopenhayn called "The Shakeout" (1993).

"The Shakeout" is a simple principle. During the growth period of the ILC many organizations join the market without differentiating factors – the market fattens up because the overall market value is on the rise, so people join to enjoy the spoils – causing an overflow of suppliers once the demand begins to mature and level out. Hopenhayn believes that "The Shakeout" hasn't actually happened until the amount of suppliers is less than 70 per cent of the volume at its peak. With this in mind, and given the current state of the social media industry (specifically in the UK), I'd say we're due to lose about 30 per cent of the suppliers over the next 18 months or so as the market matures and levels out.

While this sounds terrifying, it's simply market forces acting naturally. However, there is a way to break the trend of the ILC and access a new market at the bottom of a new curve.

Six months ago I was reading the *Harvard Business Review* and I stumbled upon an article by Tim Breene and Paul Nunes, both of Accenture, who were promoting their book *Jumping the S-Curve* (2011). Breene and Nunes are interested in helping their clients to break the cycle of decline and "leap" onto the next s-curve and by providing a methodology for innovation, they hope to

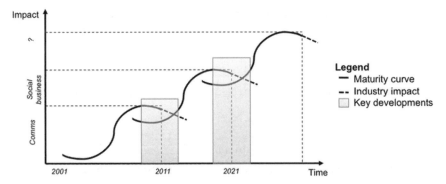

Figure 10.3: Industry life cycle analysis of social media industry

help many organizations "buck" the decline of the PLC. After spending a considerable amount of time looking at how Klepper had applied the PLC to the ILC, I began to try and overlay some of my thinking to Breene and Nunes' model. The results of which are highlighted in Figure 10.3.

Here we see three s-curves, each representing a period of around ten years. For the first curve, I've taken Figure 10.2 and begun to look at what and when the next curve could be. Given that the last few years has seen the original innovators (Brian Solis, Jeff Dachis, David Armano and so on) from curve one begin to discuss social business, it's a fair guess to say that the next ten years is going to see social business becoming a large part of the industry. It will be the innovation that the industry needs to sustain itself.

It's a difficult leap, but it will act as a filter and force true innovation amongst suppliers and the potential rewards (i.e. market volume) are, in my opinion, far greater than anything that the industry has seen over the past ten years.

Social business

Every business is, in some shape or form, a social business. It relies on a simple process of creating a product or service and then selling it. To sell that product or service, you need to communicate what it is to the people that may buy it. You also need to communicate with everyone in the organization to ensure that they understand what the product or service is and why people might buy it. So, in this sense, communication is a fundamental part of business, as it's a fundamental part of being a human. So every business is social.

But, however social the principles of businesses are, organizations are still slow to move and in a hyper-connected world, this is presenting a series of issues:

1. Increasingly empowered consumers.
2. Increasingly geographically disparate and departmentalized employees.
3. A lack of organizational agility or adaptiveness.

In my (humble) opinion, many organizations could resolve these issues by using social technologies and processes.

The modern consumer has changed – prior to digital technology, our network of friends would be fairly local and our experiences would be shaped by that network. Robin Dunbar proposed that the number of meaningful relationships that we could hold at any time was around 150, it would be easy to suggest that with the rise of social networks such as Facebook and Twitter this number has increased, but I would argue that it hasn't. We still maintain a similar number of meaningful relationships, but the dynamics of these relationships have changed and our number of "weak tie" relationships has increased giving us greater access to wider networks that transcend geography. Where my network used to be contained by Nottinghamshire, it is now global. (Of course the converse of this argument is that by spreading our network wider we become less intimately connected, but I would seriously challenge this as social media allows us to connect on a more frequent – and often more intimate – basis.)

Over the past ten years networks of people have become much more dynamic but it seems to be only recently that people are beginning to realize the effect that this change has on their lives. The scale for the potential reach of word of mouth has dramatically increased because we've become hyper-connected and our networks have widened.

The effect that this has on business is that a negative or positive brand experience used to be passed around in the village church or the pub and it would reach a single (but strong) network. However, the rise of communica-

Businesses are built on communication and the relationship between supplier and buyer, and that relationship is becoming much more open because they're communicating more often.

tions technologies and weak-tie networks means that that experience can have travelled across the globe in a matter of minutes. And this power-shift hasn't gone unnoticed.

The empowerment of the consumer now means that businesses need to be more responsive to their audience. Businesses are built on communication and the relationship between supplier and buyer, and that relationship is becoming much more open because they're communicating more often.

One of the reasons for this is the breakdown of professional and personal lives. As our networks of weak ties become wider and communication across borders increases, it's much easier for our networks to blur. Where we once had very defined boundaries between who we socialized with at the weekend and who we worked with, we now have merged networks. Or, an alternative way of looking at it is the shift from social networks to interest networks (but that's a conversation for another book). What this also means is that every employee of an organization is now a spokesperson and the ease with which a message can reach a large audience means that internal communications and a singular brand message have never been so important.

Each of the two diagrams in Figure 10.4 represents the communications flow inside an organization, but one is pre-social media and one is post-social media. The most important point to take from these diagrams is that where we once used to control the external brand touch points (public relations, advertising, customer service) we now have every department exposed to the outside world in some shape or form.

This breaching of communications barriers means that it has never been as important to create a cohesive brand message. Businesses have attempted to create unified brand messaging for years and struggled because too many external agencies interpret the message and communicate that in their own ways. But now, in addition to external agencies communicating on behalf of an organization, we have every employee doing so too.

This is where social technology can play a major role in business. By engaging with all staff in a "flat" way (every member of staff receiving the same brand message at the same time) we can begin to combat the "multiple

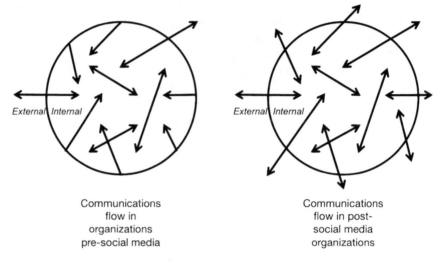

Communications
flow in
organizations
pre-social media

Communications
flow in post-
social media
organizations

Figure 10.4: Communications flows

brand message disease" that confuses consumers too frequently. After all, a consumer sees a brand, not individual departments or external agencies (when was the last time that you heard someone outside of the communications industry say, "that was a great piece of work from the digital agency"). We've already become more connected on the outside of the business, so now the challenge is to become more connected on the inside, and then we can begin to become more agile and responsive to our customers' needs.

I was introduced to the idea of the agile business by Tim Malbon, a co-founder at Made by Many, who got me thinking about the iterative brand and how we can beg, borrow and steal from the software industry to create better, more connected brands. This idea of the agile business has been popular for a long time now, but what social media is doing is forcing the hand of business to *become* more agile and more responsive.

This is one of the greatest challenges in this changing landscape – businesses have been built with scale in mind rather than innovation or creativity and this makes them very, very slow to move or react to market changes. But the empowerment of the consumer and the employee now means that business needs to react quickly and, as Brian Solis believes, use social media and mobile media to become more adaptive. Social media and social business doesn't mean having to have a Twitter stream or using Yammer. It means having an understanding about what impact this new information and these new communication lines have on a business. Even on a basic level, using the conversations that take place in a forum to help understand brand perceptions and add to existing research is an effective way of becoming more social as a business. The challenge, however, remains the same.

One of the other major challenges to organizations becoming more responsive is that businesses have built departments and these departments have become silos. We no longer work for a brand, we work for our department. I do my job to deliver my outputs, I create this web site for this web site's sake, I draft my social media strategy for my department. In an environment where the consumer sees only a single brand, we've created a culture of hundreds of ants rather than a single millipede.

> In an environment where the consumer sees only a single brand, we've created a culture of hundreds of ants rather than a single millipede.

Social business strategies

This is probably the work-in-progress section to this chapter. I've been working with a few brands for the past 12 months to re-engineer how their models work and to open up additional revenue streams as well as reconnect them (in both a passive and active way) to their audience. However, in my experience, social business is not about having a single model. As with social media in a communications perspective, there is no silver bullet.

One of the most important aspects of conducting a project that is this ambitious is ensuring that the project is manned by T-shaped people. Nathan Williams, a senior consultant at Wolff Olins, introduced me to the concept of the T-shaped person more than a year ago and it has stuck with me ever since. The T-shape approach was coined by Bill Moggridge, the CEO of IDEO, and it describes people with a breadth of multiple skills (the horizontal aspect of the T) but also with a specialist core passion (the vertical aspect of the T). In my opinion, this type of person should be perfectly suited to working with organizations to create a social business strategy.

As social business can span the whole organization, it's important to understand the structure and functional make-up of the business. To begin to solve certain issues, the depth of knowledge in a certain area is incredibly important. But the empathy and understanding that a breadth of knowledge brings is just as important and allows for greater innovation, and hopefully greater impact.

A large part of my work is to develop frameworks for complex processes. So while there are no silver bullets for social business, it is possible to build a loose framework around the processes that make up using social media as a creative and innovative tool to re-engineer business strategy.

The framework outlined below is intentionally vague as this allows it to be modified and added to dependent on the situation.

Immersion

The first step is to completely immerse yourself within the company. Before you begin to make changes it's important to understand the organization from a cultural, organizational and structural and political perspective.

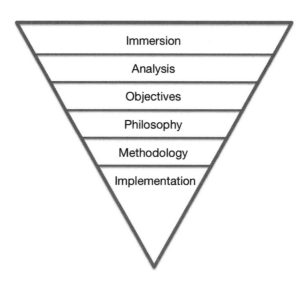

Figure 10.5: Social business strategy

Analysis

Building an acute understanding of the organization should help to create a "snagging list" of issues. This list can then be filtered into a priority matrix such as the Eisenhower Matrix (there are many, many different approaches to mapping and analysing issues, but I've found the Eisenhower Matrix to provide the most pragmatic and translatable approach).

Objectives

Working with the organization to create a list of key objectives, we can borrow from Darrell Mann's *Hands on Systematic Innovation* (2002) and begin by looking for the ideal final result (IFR), as this should help to force the organization to focus on much more specific solutions and identify wider issues at the same time.

Philosophy

Creating a philosophy around the change will sound like a shout back to the 1990s when organizational change was more about thinking than doing. However, this process involves communicating with a variety of different business cultures and it's important to create an overarching philosophy that translates the processes being carried out into something meaningful for everyone.

Methodology

Realistically, this should be the easiest part. Using the depth of knowledge that you've built in social media should enable you to create a systematic approach to drafting a strategy and selecting the correct tools for the job.

Implementation

This is often the most forgotten phase, but undeniably the most important. Whether you're managing the implementation or carrying it out as a supplier, it's important to remain as close to the project as possible to ensure that the IFRs are met as closely as possible.

This framework is still a very basic outline of how to approach social business and I would love to open this up to a wider discussion over the next few years. After all, we're at the start of the s-curve, so we have a couple of years to perfect it before everyone else catches up and we get another "Shakeout".

Roundup

Want more? See what has been said about this chapter or get involved and discuss it with the author and other readers on our LinkedIn group, find it by visiting http://www.socialmedia-mba.com or search for "The Social Media MBA Alumni".

The challenge for businesses around the world is to become more connected – to their workforce and their consumer.

By widening the brand network, you'll help your company become smarter, more responsive and more profitable. After all, would you rather buy a meal at a restaurant where you've designed the meal, spoken to the chef and met the maître d' or buy a pre-packed sandwich from a faceless supermarket where even the cashier interaction has been removed?

Using social media shouldn't be about ticking a box, but an opportunity to re-think your business.

In the next chapter Max Tatton-Brow takes this one step further and also asks you to re-think your advocates.

Acknowledgements

It's not exactly customary to write acknowledgements at the end of a chapter, but the internet (and specifically social media) is a karmic-ecosystem and none of my ideas would've been possible without some incredible inspiration, support and general amazingness. Ged Carroll for hours and hours of telephone chats, Mat Morisson for being an anchor and an inspiration, the all round fantastic Tim Hoang, Rebecca Caddy for listening to everything I've spouted about ever, Tim Malbon for introducing me to the concept of agile, Stephen Waddington for biz chat and martinis, Nathan Williams for forcing me to be smarter, Brian Solis for his thoughts on adaptive business, my old family at Wolfstar Consultancy (but specifically Mark Hanson, Mike Cooper, Tim Sinclair and Stuart Bruce), my new family at VCCP (Dominic Stinton,

Graham Drew, Tracey Follows and Amelia Torode), Gabbi Cahane, Philip Sheldrake and all the guys at Meanwhile and Antony Mayfield for influencing almost everything in my professional life.

References

Hopenhayn, H.A. (1993) The shakeout. Economics Working Papers 33, Department of Economics and Business, Universitat Pompeu Fabra.

Klepper, S. (1997) Industry life cycles. *Industrial and Corporate Change*, 6 (1), Carnegie Mellon University, PA, USA (http://www.vwl.uni-mannheim.de/stahl/!/van/fss07/ Literature/10_LifeCycle/KleS_indlc.pdf).

Levitt, T. (1965) *Exploit the Product Lifecycle.* Graduate School of Business Administration, Harvard University.

Mann, D. (2002) *Hands on Systematic Innovation.* CREAX Press.

Nunes, P. and Breene, T. (2011) *Jumping the S Curve: How to Beat the Growth Cycle, Get on Top, and Stay There.* Harvard Business School Press.

Nunes, P. and Breene, T. (2011) Reinvent your business before it's too late. *Harvard Business Review*, 101, 79–83

Rogers, E.M. (1962) (Revised edition 1983) *Diffusion of Innovations.* Glencoe, IL: Free Press.

Chapter 11

How to handle your VIIPs, QIIPs and LIIPs

Max Tatton-Brown

In short

- How to prioritize, manage and take control of your brand advocates online.
- Insight into how a little B2B perspective can now benefit any strategy.
- A consideration of the rising cost for consumers to "Like" one more brand.

Overview

In this chapter, Max Tatton-Brown, Account Manager at top ten UK tech PR agency, EML Wildfire (www.emlwildfire.com/) clarifies the shifting tectonics of the advocate opportunity – looking at how you can harness an increasingly powerful public and confront what comes next when the old tricks of social media wear off.

The chapter is designed to give your neurons a good crack round the chops, no matter what your level of experience, and get you thinking about aspects of creating advocates that you haven't yet considered.

The "bad" news

It's commonly suggested that because of social channels, brands are more vulnerable today than they have ever been. For better or worse, the days of influencers wearing a hat with "PRESS" tucked into the rim and filing stories every 24 hours are a distant memory.

The verbal assassination of your brand is now a constant, inevitable and very public reality. For many, this has been a painful slap in the face – others have taken it as a wake-up call.

Either way, we now live in a world where one man sticks a YouTube video up because your airline smashed his guitar and the reputational damage echoes across the world. The barriers between online and offline influence are crumbling.

The good news

But (luckily) it swings both ways. If social media has empowered citizens, then this includes their ability to very publicly support the brands they appreciate. Peer recommendation is still the number one influencer on buying decisions, both in B2C and B2B. And it's now up for grabs.

At the risk of this turning into a "choose your own adventure" book, if you're already comfortable with the basis for advocate strategy, you might want to skip to ahead to the part about VIIPs, QIIPs and LIIPs. The rest of the class and I will join you there when we're done with the basics.

The advocate opportunity

When conversations were offline only, any potential insights were scattered and hidden in pubs, kitchens and offices across the land. The closest brands could get to monitoring sentiment was expensive, time-consuming and artificial market research. The true views and opinions were out in the field but frustratingly inaccessible.

This has now changed. Feedback bellows from every channel, made intelligible only by smart strategy and some nifty tools. You can see who's recommending your work and flying the flag for your brand. Finally, at least some of your advocates can be catalogued and understood.

This is obviously the first opportunity which presents itself; above and before all else, it's time to start building a better picture of your customers. Build strong links into your customer relationship management strategy to create the most complete picture possible or create a Google Doc if your needs are more basic. Don't forget to make sure this link works both ways. Whenever you're reaching out to customers through traditional channels, never miss an opportunity to poll them for social network accounts. You never know what you might find. Once you have an idea of this landscape, it's time to take the next steps.

Make it easy

Traditionally, brands have been quite happy to bandy their power around and call the shots. And customers have been in a state of Stockholm syndrome, blithely accepting their fate. But today, a lighter touch will pay off.

The key is to concentrate on making it as easy as possible for advocates to express their feelings toward the brand and provide as many interesting and stimulating opportunities as you can. On the most basic level, this can be as simple as just having an active and responsive presence on networks where your customers will expect to see it. Or as adventurous as cleverly pitched competitions whereby they can create content on channels where they might not have expected to find you.

> . . . you have to put some good hard thought into the question they'll be asking themselves: what's in it for me?

But especially with this second option, you have to put some good hard thought into the question they'll be asking themselves: what's in it for me?

Incentives

What's interesting (and sometimes challenging) here is the incentive. Ideally, it should be prestige or something intangible that builds a longer and deeper affinity with the brand.

Once you start throwing iPads at the problem, you're appealing to greed. By all means stick it into the strategy but only if you're aware that it's a quick, shallow and often superficial victory. If you just want a bigger follower number so as to be taken more seriously then maybe there's value.

But remember, good social strategy builds long-term, sustainable relationships. That takes time, practice and ideally a genuine interest in your customer.

Up to here, I've concentrated on advocates in the broadest sense. But how does the theory hold up when you mainly sell straight to businesses?

B2B

In social marketing, B2B gets a hard time. Some will stick their hand in the air and insist that it has no place or the audience isn't interested. Others will mumble something about LinkedIn.

What's great about advocate strategy is that it's the perfect example of where, properly integrated, B2B social media can really come into its own. Partly for the advantages we've discussed but also because of how it can affect the culture. For example, how well do you really listen to your customers? Are they complaining more than you thought?

What's more, as more consumers become small self-interested reputation businesses building blogs and profiles online, I think every brand could learn something from the B2B philosophy to social strategy.

B2B reputation

In the B2B area, it's worth remembering that the benefits *for the advocate* can be doubly important too. Rather than a simple sense of esteem by association with a ketchup brand, it's a way to demonstrate your professionalism and industry knowledge.

For this audience, there are some great opportunities to bring in LinkedIn as a universal login. Let's say you're a software company and you want to create a community where people can share best practice or downloadable scripts for others to rate. Integrating prestige from activity with their social identity allows them to accumulate and demonstrate it more widely and appropriately. At the same time, the exposure of your brand on their LinkedIn profile introduces a new path of discovery for potential community members.

In B2B, these advocates will often build their own reputation by valiantly defending their decision to pick your product over the rest. If someone asks for a recommendation, you want to make it as easy as possible for them to be aware of it and respond to it. But be aware that this is also increasingly true as individuals build their reputations among peers in the consumer space too.

A case study of a successful B2B initiative is described by Hans Notenboom, Global Director B2B Online at Phillips, in Chapter 18.

In this next section, I'll be looking more closely at how we can break influencers out into these groups and the ramifications for your strategy.

VIIPs, QIIPs and LIIPs

For as long as networks of social connections have existed, online and off, some individuals have always been naturally linked into larger communities than others. The strength and number of these connections offer the fundamental synapses through which messages spread on social networks. Therefore, those with more connections can pose both a greater threat as a critic and greater asset as an advocate.

But when it comes to strategy, we need something a bit more detailed and nuanced than this to go on. We already know that users behave in different ways, so how do we classify them to help prioritize and nurture a community of advocates?

The VIIPs

The first group we'll be looking at has the most conventional label – probably because they're closest to what brands have embraced through other channels over the years.

They're not the guy with a pocket full of business cards, schmoozing the room as you might expect – they're the ones you remember without a card because they knew interesting things and could tell a good story. But more than that, they are the ones who make a strong and stimulating connection with people.

This group will tend to create and inject content into the echo chamber of the networks. They may blog. They may publish YouTube videos. Perhaps they even do something in real life which means they are a primary source of content or information in that area, i.e. game developer, serial entrepreneur or washed up Hollywood actor.

This aspect, in which they stand apart from the other groups, is actually quite traditional. Since the dawn of society, reputation has spread from those who create. It's just that now the creation can be anything from a thought-provoking blog of business tips to a video of a cat dressed like a ninja. It'll never be true that everyone gets their 60 seconds of fame, but the barriers to entry have certainly drooped.

Brands and VIIPs

So how does this powerful group co-exist with brands and fit into an advocate programme? Can you tame potential giant-killers?

The real question here is how best to redress the balance of power. Influencing this group isn't easy as the ball is very much in their court and it's staying there. This isn't a flash in the pan, it's the new paradigm and as time goes on, they will only realize their power more fully.

Bear in mind that often, one of the origins of their reputation is integrity. Any attempt to suggest they compromise in that area is a sure-fire shortcut to disaster. That means no bribing bloggers.

Instead, ask not what your advocate can do for you but what you can do for your advocate. In the B2B space, again, remember the value of reputation. Can you create some kind of programme to recognize their authority and reward them accordingly? Keep them close and keep them happy.

In doing so, the relationship becomes more symbiotic. Any kind of scheme like this includes an implicit acceptance of the counterpart's power. Of course, the trick is to make sure that there's sufficient incentive on the table for these most influential advocates to submit to this agreement. Would they be better off going it alone?

Stimulate your VIIPs

The other vital consideration with this group of content creators is to provide them with interesting stimuli to inspire further input into their network.

Remember, they'll often bring together elements from offline and other channels to create something for their social followers.

This means more than telling them about the wonderful new expensive advertising campaigns you're about to kick off. Show that you have considered them properly rather than as an afterthought in your strategy. They are not coverage-monkeys who will dance to your whim every time you release a YouTube video.

This prompts another interesting question: can brands also be members of this group on social networks? The answer is of course yes. This is the Holy Grail – become worth following because of independent value and a world of new doors opening up to you.

Again, this offers opportunities to shift the power differential in favour of brands. Consider inviting influencers to write on your blog or participate in a Q&A to build their own reputation. Once you have influence to distribute, you gain an asset that will grow and grow *if* you forge the right associations. Here, continuity across channels becomes important. Know who visits which channels and what they expect to find there. Don't duplicate.

So, that's the first group that brands need to be aware of, the number one priority, the most important and the most broadly and powerfully influential. Over time, expect more and more to enter its membership and be prepared to share power with them as a sort of coalition.

When I say pay them attention, I mean it almost literally. In return, you will receive the maximum return for your investment in social media and over time, careful skill will help these relationships grow and further increase in value.

And the best bit? It's cheap. The difficulty is a shift in mind and philosophy. Once that hurdle is overcome, all you're giving up is time to gain one of the most powerful tools in modern business.

Oh, and their name? Let's keep it simple. These are your VIIPs – very important and influential people. Roll out the red carpet.

The QIIPs

The second tier of advocate comes with subtle but important differences. If this is a game of "Chinese whispers" (and social marketing often is) then you're now looking at the second step in the chain.

These are your retweeters, your curators, your commenters and mentions. They spread the word. They may not have the creative spark of VIIPs but some people never do. And there are many more people who are naturally more "follower" than "leader".

The most important thing is to keep everything you produce on every channel as shareable as possible. It's with QIIPs' support that VIIPs (including brands) become kings and their content starts to zip through networks.

Don't shoot the messenger, encourage them. Often, the eagerness of this group will be such that they're more interested in passing content on than checking how much value it will actually bring to their network. Hence, the proliferation of linkbait and unverified news on Twitter.

Plant the seed and it will grow

With social media, there's often a lot of discussion around seeding – how do you get content out onto social networks so that it might eventually reach that holy adjective of phantom ROI, "viral"? From the brand perspective, part of the answer is definitely to make it as easy as possible to share.

Any work you do to get the VIIPs on side should be reflected in spreading and uptake by this second, supporting group. Indeed, one way of judging just how V a VIIP may be is to gauge the interactions they have with other groups, including retweets.

The biggest difference here is how much brands need to prioritize this group. They're by no means unimportant but even if you did spend the same amount of time on them as VIIPs, you couldn't see the same kinds of returns.

It's really this group that has helped spawn the notorious "follow and RT to win" competition. The fact of their lesser influence is probably the key reason why such competitions can only ever produce relatively superficial results. It's not so much that they don't serve a purpose, just that you can't build a campaign from them alone.

If there was some way to reproduce their virulence in VIIPs, then we might be onto something. You can bet that there are labs of social media scientists across the land trying to create such magic. The real opportunity here is for brands to harness these sharers to help you reach VIIP status. Give them

> The real opportunity here is for brands to harness these sharers to help you reach VIIP status. Give them content they can share to make themselves look intelligent and they will flock to the brand.

content they can share to make themselves look intelligent and they will flock to the brand.

Again, if you're aiming to become a B2B thought leader then whack out a few insightful "top five reasons why X" or "seven tricks to perfect Y" and the cynical among you should find a following.

So if they come just below the VIIPs in terms of both importance and influence, it only seems fair to label them accordingly; these are your QIIPs or quite important and influential people.

In many ways they offer the simplest level of endorsement which can be tracked online. Once you sink below this level of participation, advocates become more or less untraceable. But that doesn't mean they don't exist and certainly doesn't mean they should be ignored.

Let's look at the final tier – the "social submarine" of the advocate mix.

The LIIPs

In some ways, this group and its smallest obvious footprint is the most interesting. This is in no small part due to the mysteries surrounding it.

For example, you have an account with 15 followers, a small picture and no bio under the name @Jeremy_Warner55. Doesn't give us a lot to work with, does it.

Now think of Jeremy like an iceberg. Instead of bisection by water level, you have the membrane between online and offline influence. As we've established, offline influence exists but is hard to measure (some would argue the same can be said for online, but that's a story for another chapter).

The key is to remember that you are never seeing the whole picture. What appears to be a molehill in the digital world can disguise decades of accumulated offline reputation beneath the surface.

So what are we to do?

These days (and for the most part, quite rightly) the focus in social media is on interactions. A newsfeed linked to Twitter, Facebook and LinkedIn just doesn't cut it – you need to be in there, getting your hands dirty and starting conversations.

But this group won't be part of those (at least, for now). Therefore, while you'll be making a good impression on them when they see the conversations, they're a big part of the reasoning behind getting the balance right with pure content creation too.

They may be your biggest fans in real life but just dipping their toe in the water of social media. Tell them something they don't know. Everyone focuses on making sure people can share with social networks but this lot may be more likely to email something on – certainly considering that their friends might be of similar or inferior social competency.

However, the fact remains that, in the short term, their overall contribution to your social strategy can only be less than the other groups. Even if some QIIPs are fakers with little overall influence, they'll still be passing the message on more effectively and contributing more to your goals.

Strategically, the best you can hope for here is to keep introducing easy ways for them to increase their influence. In the B2B world, this may mean blogging about how they can master social networks or about the benefits. If you help them become more competent in this area, you'll gain a respect and gratitude from them that is hard to generate through other means.

In short, avoid a Titanic situation. Objects may be closer (and more dangerous) than they appear. Take them seriously, never write them off.

I hope I've emphasized that these people aren't unimportant, just less important. Making them – your LIIPs – less important and influential people.

However, we live in a fast-moving world. For the third and final section of this chapter, I want to take a look at the changes, challenges and opportunities on the horizon with these groups.

What's next, how's it going to affect your business and why?

Brand mutualization, fatigue and Generation S

While writing this chapter, I leaned across to a girl in Caffé Nero and asked what she thought about "Liking" brands on Facebook and welcoming them into her newsfeed.

After a little reassurance that the enquiry was strictly for the purposes of research, she told me about a certain fashion brand and how delighted she was to see weekly deals dropped into her awareness so conveniently.

A common sentiment, you can imagine. So I continued to ask how open she would be to following another brand and receiving even more deals in a similar fashion. Fairly open, she thought. "How about another?", I asked, "and what if it shows up instead of the latest story from your best friend?"

She sort of reached the same questions I hope you're mulling now. How many brands can one person follow? What's the cost? At what point does curation of content in your feed clash with conservation of messages from your social graph?

With every poster on the tube these days imploring you to "Like" them on Facebook or follow them on Twitter, where do diminishing returns set in for the user? When do they actually start to resent it? It's early days right now and the novelty alone is often enough to get your foot in the door.

But as time goes on, how do you persuade your customers to follow you instead of the competition? How do you maintain your importance if you're the incumbent brand? How do you avoid them "Liking" you but then silencing your messages in their feed, rendering them phantom fans in your stats?

> . . . as time goes on, how do you persuade your customers to follow you instead of the competition?

If you aren't asking these questions yet, it's time to start.

Next generation

At best, today's social situation is in a state not too dissimilar to puberty. Brands' voices are breaking and they're questioning who they are and who they want to be when they grow up.

Forgivingly, much of the same advice still applies – your peers are in the same situation. And that means both competitors and customers. Consumers are growing into a mantle of power and maturity – some cautiously finding their influence in the world and others lashing out for attention.

But, on the horizon, a new generation is approaching for whom dominant social network brands will be as familiar as McDonalds and Nike. This generation Like brands voraciously, expressing themselves through their affiliations as teenagers have for decades now. The Kurt Cobain t-shirt of yesteryear has been replaced with a Nirvana Facebook page. Only, today, it provides free advertising for the Greatest Hits album.

Will they be numb and accepting of this? Will they grow up and shed the affiliations, turning to phenomena like white-walling to conserve their privacy? Or will they accept the Zuckerberg age, embrace an online life and with it offer brands the easy advocates and VIIPs they think they're on the cusp of controlling?

And what of new options like Google+, in which they could segment the brands out of their everyday feed into specific "Circles"? Has the search giant introduced a way for everyone to have their cake and eat it?

Time will tell, and no doubt we'll find out together.

Roundup

Want more? See what has been said about this chapter or get involved and discuss it with the author and other readers on our LinkedIn group, find it by visiting http://www.socialmedia-mba.com or search for "The Social Media MBA Alumni".

In these early days of social media, not all advocates are born equal. Whether it's because they're late to the party or simply because of their personality, some have more maturely developed networks than others. And they all use them in different ways.

So consider Max's idea of VIIPs, QIIPs and LIIPs – how do these fit your audience? How do they fit you? Is it clear what's in it for them?

Hopefully, what has been discussed so far will have you thinking more clearly about the ways you can prioritize, manage and take control of your brand advocates online.

It doesn't take cash, it doesn't take massive brand power, it just takes a little careful thought and understanding of people. If it's not you, hire those who can give you this, not just in job titles with "social" in them (which I pray will disappear soon) but throughout your organization.

Part IV

Case Studies

Chapter 12

Kerry McGuire-Balanza, Director of Strategic Marketing

The author

Kerry McGuire-Balanza, Director of Strategic Marketing leads ARM's digital marketing team. With more than 11 years of ARM experience, Kerry brings a unique partnership perspective to ARM's digital marketing strategy. Follow her @ARMMobile and on the Smart Mobile Devices blog.

The company

The ARM business model is unique as they license their semiconductor intellectual property (IP) to a huge number of Partners, primarily semiconductor manufacturers and original equipment manufacturers (OEMs). These Partners rely on ARM's IP to design high performance, low power processors that lie at the heart of a variety of devices, including smartphones, tablet PCs, digital set-top boxes, smart meters and internet connected devices. At present, ARM technology powers a large share of internet connected devices, including over 90 per cent of the world's smartphones and tablets.

ARM work collaboratively with 250 licensees, who manufacture ARM-based semiconductor chips, and with over 800 ARM Connected Community (CC) partners who support ARM-based products in the market.

In Q1 2011 approximately 1,800 employees delivered more than $180 million in revenue and shipments of over 1.8 billion ARM-based processors.

Our social media strategy

The key objective with social media is to build industry awareness of ARM technology, and partner innovations powered by ARM technology, through unique, authentic digital content and conversations. Social media enables ARM to support our partners' dialogue and give voice to those innovative partner companies who have yet to develop their own digital footprint.

Our strategy is to activate and integrate conversations with targeted stakeholders across all our social media channels. To achieve this we created an ARM presence on YouTube, Twitter and an internally developed blog network.

Our YouTube videos found on our ARMflix channel serve as rich visual content to support all of our social media outlets. Our blog communities and Twitter handles work together to initiate and support a rich conversation. Because of our broad industry presence, we have used our core business markets to segment our content and target our audiences better. This strategy enables our followers to find and follow only the content best suited to their interests.

For example, those most interested in emerging mobile devices follow the Smart Mobile Device community blog and @ARMMobile on Twitter. While those most interested in the broader embedded market, follow the Embedded community blog and @ARMEmbedded.

In addition, ARM directly hosts the ARMFan Facebook page and supports a LinkedIn "ARM Based Group", which is managed and sustained by external individuals with strong interests in ARM technology.

ARM's social media strategy and execution is driven within corporate communications by a small team in Austin Texas and in partnership with PR firm Racepoint Group. The real key to our success is broad internal support for content generation. Engineers, researchers and marketing professionals across ARM create great content not only for Western markets but also in key global markets such as China. Additionally, our Connected Community team works closely with our partner companies on developing contributions to further highlight exciting innovations using ARM technology.

A recent social media success story

Background

Collaboration is a fundamental part of ARM's business model, so it seemed natural to involve our partners in our social marketing activities.

Campaign objective

The goal of our campaign was to demonstrate the pervasiveness of the ARM technology by highlighting innovative ARM-powered partner products. Mutual benefit was a key objective. ARM partners benefit through broad exposure across ARM's digital channels and ARM benefits by being able to demonstrate the relationship between ARM technology and our partners' products. In the short term, we hoped to achieve a direct increase in audience and dialogue. In the longer term, we hoped to strengthen our relationship and engagement with our partners.

Delivery

For ARMflix, ARM organized a small internal video team that captured partner technology demos and interviews at key industry trade shows. This video content was featured on ARMflix and highlighted within our community blogs: check out our CES, Mobile World Congress and Embedded World coverage.

To expand ARM's blog content, ARM formalized guidelines to enable partners to submit a guest partner blog and then worked with partners on content submissions. Accepted submissions were published in our blog communities and promoted on the ARM.com homepage. In Q1 2011 we published double the number of partner blogs over the previous quarter. We even featured a guest partner blog from iControl Networks when we launched our new Embedded Community in March.

Twitter remains one of our best tools for spreading ARM and partner news. @ARMCommunity is our most popular Twitter handle and helped to drive our engagement to its highest level in March where we had over

40,000 bit.ly clicks. A number of partners have even adopted #ARM to highlight their ARM related product news.

Budget

As a small team with lots of energy and industry friends plus a little travel budget, a couple of good tools and a supportive PR firm, ARM relies primarily on internal teams to film, blog and tweet. We use standard tools for distribution and analysis.

ROI

In the short term we are tracking direct audience growth (followers, fans, members and subscribers) and engagement (blog views, video views, bit.ly clicks and so on). In Q1 our subscriber audience grew more than 20 per cent over Q4 and our direct engagement is a healthy eight times the size of our subscriber audience. In terms of partner engagement, ARM published 12 guest partner blogs in Q1: double the amount from previous quarters.

Key learnings

- Don't be afraid to expand collaboration within your community to your partners and customers.

By allowing others to mutually benefit from our social media efforts, ARM has greatly increased both the breadth and frequency of our social media content.

Kerry's best advice

- Just start! You can start small with just a blog or a simple Twitter handle.
- Know your audience! If you have lots of great content to share, consider segmenting your content so that it is focused on your key audiences and easily to find.

- Think integrated! Leverage your channels together for the best impact and ROI.
- Keep trying! Social media is rapidly changing, so should we. Don't be afraid of change.

Want more? See what has been said about this case or get involved and discuss it with the author and other readers on our LinkedIn group, find it by visiting http://www.socialmedia-mba.com or search for "The Social Media MBA Alumni".

Chapter 13

Jan Gooding, Global Marketing Director

The author

Jan Gooding is the Global Marketing Director at insurance group Aviva. She has spent over 25 years in the marketing and advertising industry, including holding senior positions at BT and British Gas, and setting up her own consultancy.

The company

Aviva is the world's sixth largest insurance group and the biggest in the UK, operating in 28 countries with 45,000 employees serving 53.4 million customers.

Aviva offers a range of financial services – from life and general insurance to pensions and asset management – and announced an IFRS operating profit of £2.55 billion for the 12 months ending 31 December 2010.

Aviva has committed to deliver one distinctive experience for our customers, wherever we are in the world – to make each customer feel that "no one recognizes me like Aviva".

Our social media strategy

The financial services industry has typically been slow to embrace social media, and until recently, Aviva was no exception. However, in 2010 the business recognized that social media presented the opportunity to build relationships and deep interactions with its customers and stakeholders. As a global brand, Aviva has taken a big step forward by creating and maintaining an ongoing presence on a number of social media platforms.

Our intention was to create interactive and engaging opportunities for consumers to come into contact with the Aviva brand outside of the annual purchase or renewal process, in a way that displayed our brand promise of individual recognition.

To kick-start this effort, Aviva embedded social media into its first ever global brand campaign – "You are the Big Picture" (YATBP). This brought to life the brand promise by featuring real stories of customers, employees, business partners and communities, via a high profile and impactful PR and advertising campaign.

The YATBP campaign broke new ground for both Aviva and the financial services industry, by having a strong social media element at its heart. YATBP used social media both to deliver awareness for the campaign amongst key consumer audiences and to facilitate key pillars of the consumer-facing campaign activity. Thanks to its extensive use of social media, the YATBP campaign, and the subsequent development and interaction with Aviva's new online communities, helped us to reach new customers in new ways, providing fertile ground for forging longer term relationships. Aviva's social media strategy is closely linked to the company's wider brand activity, and is managed by the central team in the London group centre.

Recent social media success story

Background

YATBP, Aviva's first global brand campaign, featured real stories of the people most important to Aviva – customers, employees, business partners and communities. It used a range of innovative approaches to bring to life Aviva's brand promise that "no-one recognizes you like Aviva".

YATBP ran in five countries around the world, driving significant increases in brand consideration and a strong response from the public.

Our strategy put social media at the heart by encouraging public participation, as a way to demonstrate that we live up to the democratic values and individual recognition that were at the heart of the campaign. It enabled Aviva not just to recognize a handful of exceptional people, but also to recognize and engage tens of thousands of people across the world.

Delivery

We did this by inviting members of the public to donate a photo for a chance to have their image projected onto a landmark building in one of five global cities. In return, Aviva pledged to give £1 for every photo donated to support Aviva's Street to School charity programme. More than 59,000 photos were uploaded by members of the public, both through our campaign hub and via the Facebook page.

ROI

In total, 1.8 million people visited the campaign's online hub from 160 countries around the world, and Aviva was able to grow an active Facebook community of 57,000 within just two months.

Meanwhile, we streamed the projection of photos via YouTube – the first examples of YouTube live streaming ever to be delivered on this scale, generating more than 68,000 views. We also joined in on Twitter to celebrate with the members of the public who had their photos projected, and to tell them more about the campaign.

Key learnings

Financial services as a sector has been comparatively slow to adopt social media, but Aviva's experience has demonstrated that people are happy to engage with an insurance brand online – as long as the campaign is based on shared values and presents a relatable, human face to the world.

Jan's best advice

Above all, we would advise other brands to make sure that their social media is relevant. Wherever possible, brands should make the user themselves the centrepiece of their campaign – people will engage much more deeply with a brand that shows they listen to and recognize their consumers: joining up the messages and tone of voice on all the platforms and channels to create a consistent user experience.

Want more? See what has been said about this case or get involved and discuss it with the author and other readers on our LinkedIn group, find it by visiting http://www.socialmedia-mba.com or search for "The Social Media MBA Alumni".

Chapter 14

DELL

Stuart Handley, Communications Director, EMEA, LATAM and Canada

The author

Stuart is Communications Director for Dell. He has worked for the company since November 2007 and is responsible for the company's Public Relations and Corporate Communications across EMEA, LATAM and Canada.

The company

For more than 25 years, Dell has played a critical role in transforming computing, enabling more affordable and more pervasive access to technology worldwide. Today, the computer industry is at a critical inflection point that will redefine the types of products and services customers demand from their technology providers. Dell is addressing this industry change, listening to customers and using that insight to create innovative technology solutions that help them succeed. Dell has annual revenues of over $60 billion and approximately 100,000 employees across 180 countries.

Our social media strategy

Word of mouth can be the best publicity. It can also be the worst. Millions of voices across the social media landscape go unheard and unanswered every day. The challenge facing brands is how to actively listen to those conversations, learn from them and then engage.

There is an average of 25,000 conversations online everyday about Dell. This makes Dell one of the most talked about brands on the social web. These conversations span everything from an opinion or suggestion on a product or service, to complaints and information that others will find useful or fun.

Dell's heritage of direct customer connections and online leadership are the seeds of our early adoption and drive to connect with customers via social media. From a cultural and leadership perspective the business needed little convincing of the need for investment in the resources and tools required to guide, monitor and support these efforts.

> Engaging in honest, **direct conversations** with customers and stake-holders is a part of who we are, who we've always been. The social web amplifies our opportunity to listen and learn and invest ourselves in two-way dialogue, enabling us to become a better company with more to offer the people who depend on us.
>
> *Michael Dell*

The evolution of listening

Dell took its first steps to formalize an approach to monitoring customer conversations in 2006, with the formation of the Community Outreach Team. Tech support experts were hand selected for their problem solving expertise and superior interpersonal skills. Soon this outreach expanded beyond tech support to encompass all bloggers that commented about the company. Several years later Dell appointed two chief listeners to oversee the company's monitoring and outreach efforts. In 2010 Dell began to offer customer support through Facebook and launched the @Dellcares Twitter account to offer 24/7 global support coverage in English as well as customer support outreach in ten other languages.

Most recent success story: social media ground control

Background

In the spring of 2010, Dell launched its global Social Media Ground Control team to monitor, measure and report on Dell social media activities. They also help with the operational side of listening at Dell. The social media teams embedded across the company continue to be empowered to assist customers in need, engage with their fans, build brand advocates and create powerful relationships with our customers. In December 2010, Dell launched the company's Social Media Listening Command Center, the operational hub for the Global Social Media Ground Control team. The Social Media Listening Command Center tracks more than 25,000 daily topic posts related to Dell and mentions on Twitter that together have a reach greater than the circulation of the top 12 daily newspapers in the United States. Dell's ability to listen and quickly learn about hot issues has been invaluable.

Delivery

The engine behind the Social Media Listening Command Center is Radian6 – a complete platform allowing Dell to listen, measure and engage across the entire social web. Dell's Social Media and Community team in partnership with Radian6 has customized this platform and implemented the aggregation of information and intelligence to systematically track conversations across 'the web and around the world.

The aggregation of this information and the insights from conversations can include information such as trending across topics, sentiment, geographies and share of voice. Four central screens display real-time information on:

- **Influencers** – shows the top influential authors within a selected topic.
- **Geographies** – shows the geographic distribution of Twitter posts within a topic.
- **Priorities** – shows the volume of posts for a selected topic.
- **Summary** – shows a summary of activity within the selected topic.

Listening is important, but engagement is also critical. Dell now reaches out directly to around 10,000 customers per week. The tools we have in place allow us to closely monitor the change in tonality of conversations (from negative to neutral and neutral to positive) we are able to achieve by engaging with people through social media channels. Currently a significant percentage of the interactions lead to an immediate upswing in tonality, demonstrating a direct influence on brand perception and customer experience.

ROI

- Over 25,000 conversations tracked online everyday about Dell in 11 languages and collated into actionable reports.
- Support team – over 10,000 direct customer interactions per week.
- Positive impact on customer satisfaction scores – significant conversion of demoters to promoters.
- Positive impact on call centre traffic.
- Improvement in repeat purchase rates.
- Higher purchase rate from customers who engage via social media communities.

Key learnings

- The creation of the Social Media Listening Command Center has been one major step in the drive to embed social media and active listening and engagement across the business. By embedding social media listening across every business unit and functional unit, Dell is allowing each team to have the capability to engage directly with customers.
- Social media gives Dell more opportunities to listen, connect and engage than ever before. More than 9,000 Dell employees are now formally trained

in social media around the world. Many are actively listening across the web as part of their jobs today, and these team members will increase in number and develop new skills in the next few years.

- The foundation of the Social Media Listening Command Center has been a significant step and gives Dell a great listening platform. That said there is still work ahead of us to become even more sophisticated in the way we monitor and engage. At Dell we firmly believe that social media represents a significant opportunity to drive brand awareness and customer loyalty, by understanding our customers better, and this means listening first and foremost. If we don't listen we can never understand our customers' needs, and it is customer need that dictates how and why they interact with Dell.

Stuart's best advice

You need to participate in online dialogue about your brand – good or bad. Social media for business is defined by listening, engaging and, critically, acting – use the insights you receive to improve your product, marketing, customer support or any other area of your business.

Want more? See what has been said about this case or get involved and discuss it with the author and other readers on our LinkedIn group, find it by visiting http://www.socialmedia-mba.com or search for "The Social Media MBA Alumni".

Chapter 15

Will Lockie, Online Marketing Manager

The author

Will is the Online Marketing Manager for Evans Cycles. Prior to joining Evans, Will worked with clients such as Toyota, Porsche and Halifax on their search and social programmes with iCrossing, a digital agency. He is IPA qualified and loves riding his bike.

Twitter: @will_lockie

The company

Founded in 1921, Evans Cycles is the UK's largest specialist cycle retailer. With 43 stores across the UK, and a steadily growing ecommerce business, the organization has benefited from the recent growth in popularity of cycling. Currently employing over 1,000 employees and generating a turnover in excess of £75 million, Evans Cycles launched their social commerce efforts in June 2010.

Our social media strategy

For Evans Cycles, social media means getting customers more involved in the products it sells, and allowing them to make better choices – be that informed through Twitter, Facebook or reading other customers' reviews, on or off site. This openness is manifested on the company's blog in features such as the "Ride it and Rate it" customer review programme, which invites positive and negative feedback on products on a public page.

Social media is also important as it allows the business to open up a conversation directly with its customers and to get across the passion the staff have for cycling.

The strategy, planning and execution, is managed by Will and a team of two others (including a full time social media executive). It was developed after a period of internal stakeholder research, which then moved into planning for various scenarios and processes involving customer service issues.

After the initial bedding in period, the business is now investigating ways to scale up its use of social media – especially in areas such as customer service. This means finding ways to allow the contact centre to directly respond to customer enquiries through Facebook and Twitter, for instance. It is also beginning to integrate stores into the social programme, through the use of location based marketing – Foursquare and Facebook Places/Deals.

A recent social media success story

Background

Prior to June 2010, Evans Cycles had no social media activity. The business knew that cyclists in general are passionate and very active online, so it was an easy decision to decide to engage with customers through social channels.

Campaign objective

The objective was to create a series of social presences that would enable customers to engage with the company by allowing them to communicate directly through a range of social channels such as a blog, Facebook and Twitter.

Further objectives were based around creating useful content that can help cyclists either make better purchasing decisions, or simply help them maintain their bike.

Budget

The budget to launch was £15,000. This covered the set up and build of the blog by digital agency iCrossing. A full time social media executive was also recruited to manage the workflow and also act in a community manager role.

Delivery

A blog was built on the Wordpress platform, designed in such a way to cover the following main areas:

- Different cycling disciplines and interests.
- The "ride it" events organized by Evans.
- Staff riders.

A Facebook page and Twitter feed were created at no cost. Evans created a content planner for the blog, and launch promotions across Facebook and Twitter. Evans also recently launched a You Tube channel, by filming a series of how to videos.

ROI

Evans Cycles measures its social effort in a number of ways. There is no simple focus on "fans" or last click revenue from these channels, as this does not give a representative picture of value delivered. Stand-alone social measurement is in its infancy, so the focus is on a wider, multichannel view of customers, for example, what percentage of Facebook fans regularly visit and purchase in store?

The effects of social media on search rankings, traffic and revenue are a more quantitative measure and particular attention is paid to this. Ultimately measurement is by more anecdotal means: are customers sharing content and recommending services? Are they engaged with Evans and giving good feedback? If these things are happening, then it suggests that the campaign is moving in the right direction.

Key learnings

Throughout the process:

- Do the homework (internal research).
- Define what social media means to the business.
- Remain flexible, try stuff, get rid of things that don't work.
- Check in with customers, ask them what they want to hear about.
- Create rules of thumb (e.g. if we find a piece of content interesting as cyclists, then probably our customers will).

Will's best advice

- Do the research first and figure out how you can be useful to your customers, know what your strategy is. This will be different for every brand.
- Know how your business internally will resource a campaign and deal with issues. Expect to make some mistakes, and be transparent when you do.
- Ask customers what they want and don't take yourselves too seriously – nothing is worse than a brand that shouts about themselves all the time.

Want more? See what has been said about this case or get involved and discuss it with the author and other readers on our LinkedIn group, find it by visiting http://www.socialmedia-mba.com or search for "The Social Media MBA Alumni".

Chapter 16

Verity Clifton, Ribena Marketing Director

The author

Verity Clifton is the Ribena Marketing Director. Verity has worked at GlaxoSmithKline (GSK) since 2005 and has held a variety of insight and marketing roles within the organization across both consumer and nutritional healthcare.

The company

The GSK company mission is to improve the quality of human life by enabling people to do more, feel better and live longer. It's one of the world's leading research-based pharmaceutical and healthcare companies. Headquartered in the UK, it's a global organization employing 96,500 people in over 100 countries, with a turnover of £28,392 million in 2010.

As well as medicines and vaccines, GSK also market other consumer healthcare products, many of which are among the market leaders, including Panadol, Aquafresh, Sensodyne and Niquitin. Within the nutritional healthcare division the company markets Lucozade, Ribena and Horlicks.

Our social media strategy

We know that consumers are starting to create their own content and conversation around brands through social media. This means that the power of peer-to-peer consumer recommendation is becoming ever more important. Our challenge as a brand is to know how to play a role in this "wikization". We can do this by creating content that can help to stimulate and steer conversation.

The first stage in our planning is to understand the online landscape for our target audience – where they are, in what numbers and how can we reach them through media or content. We then develop a scoring matrix across a number of different platforms. This helps to reconcile the different platforms in terms of measures such as reach and relevance. We also consider other benefits, including built in analytics and SEO. We then arrive at our final recommendation of platforms, in Ribena's case Facebook, Twitter, YouTube, Blog (using Wordpress) and Flickr.

The next challenge is to decide what to talk about. We explored topic areas developed from elements of the brand arrow, the product story and previous brand activity. We modelled online consumer interest in these areas using Google search volume prediction tools.

We developed a pro-active publishing plan mapped against the 2010 marketing plan but also incorporating our content topics. We acknowledged that we needed to leave room for reactive content, responding to news and popular culture.

Brass Agency has overall responsibility for strategy, management and delivery. The team on Ribena from GSK comprises brand managers, representatives from corporate communications and consumer care. The Brass agency team includes planning, creative, online PR, social media and analytics specialists.

Recent social media success story

Background

Ribena has a unique story to tell about its British blackcurrant growers that sets it apart from competitors. While the notions of quality associated with this can be influential in mum's purchasing decisions, she rarely has the opportunity to witness it firsthand. With the knowledge that loyalty and advocacy cannot be generated through ATL (above the line) alone, we conceived an approach incorporating key influencers, trusted platforms, British mums and, at the centre, the Ribena growers.

Campaign objective

The brief was to deliver the British blackcurrant goodness message to mums in a new way, which delivers deeper engagement, builds advocacy, rewards loyalty, forces brand re-appraisal and in turn drives frequency of purchase.

Budget

The total budget for the digital elements of the campaign was £250,000: this included planning, publishing and reacting across all social media channels throughout 2010, development of web site and Tales from Ribena Farm content and email communications.

Delivery

To reinforce the British blackcurrant goodness message, we took a leap into the world of social media with Tales from Ribena Farm: a multi-channel and multi-discipline campaign that exhibited how Ribena squash really is made from blackcurrants grown on British farms.

We used social media channels (Facebook, Twitter, YouTube, Flickr and the Ribena blog), our consumer database and an exclusive partnership with Mumsnet to recruit 12 families to win an exclusive weekend at a British Ribena blackcurrant farm. The event was designed around four "tales" where families took part in activities, learning how blackcurrants are grown and harvested, spotting birds and bugs with The Wildlife Trusts, finding buried treasure and making blackcurrant smoothies. The whole day was filmed and four short films were released across all our social media platforms and within a dedicated hub on Mumsnet.

ROI

We worked with the central GSK digital team to develop a model where we have three key measures:

- **Reach** – the total reach in terms of consumers of our activity.
- **Engagement** – the volume of consumers who take a positive step to "Like" us.
- **Action** – the volume of consumers who actively "comment on" or "retweet" our content.

Overall the campaign reached 650,000 people, with 4.1 million opportunities for members of the public to see any element of the campaign and 19,800 deep interactions via video views, downloads, likes and comments.

The aim of the campaign was to reach a specific audience of mums and shift key brand metrics. Pre and post research to evaluate the impact of the campaign in changing mums' perceptions of Ribena shows there have been significant shifts, particularly amongst Mumsnetters, in terms of Ribena being a "British brand" (14 point increase), "full of goodness" (9 point increase) and "great tasting" (14 point increase). There has also been a shift in brand warmth amongst existing loyalists from the Ribena database in terms of "willing to give to my children regularly" (9 point increase).

Key learnings

- Extend reach through paid for media and involve more consumers.
- Differentiate strategies for loyal audiences to encourage frequency and diversification across range.
- Continue activity in niche networks, like Mumsnet, where we can gain considerable shifts in attitude.

Verity's best advice

Have a clear strategic approach. Social media has the potential to touch a very diverse set of people and cover a wide range of opportunities and issues in an organization. It can also be conceptualized and planned in many ways, for example, is it CRM with bells on, is it the most revolutionary medium in the history of mankind?

A clear set of steps to define and develop what your strategy should be, which covers everything from platforms and content through to team responsibilities and analytics, will ensure great results.

Oh . . . and be brave!

Want more? See what has been said about this case or get involved and discuss it with the author and other readers on our LinkedIn group, find it by visiting http://www.socialmedia-mba.com or search for "The Social Media MBA Alumni".

Chapter 17

Madlen Nicolaus, Social Media Manager EAMER
(Europe, Africa and Middle East Region)

The author

Madlen Nicolaus is responsible for representing and managing Kodak's social media activities in the EAMER region. This includes strategy, content creation and speaking engagements. Her background is in the PR industry.

Twitter: @madleeeen, @Kodak_DE, @Kodak_UK

The company

As the world's foremost imaging innovator, Kodak helps consumers, businesses and creative professionals unleash the power of pictures and printing to enrich their lives.

On any given day, people worldwide take about 45 million pictures with Kodak digital cameras or Kodak film. And 40 per cent of all commercially printed materials are touched by Kodak technology. More than 75 million people worldwide manage, share and create photo gifts online at KODAK Gallery, www.kodakgallery.com. To learn more about Kodak, visit www.kodak.com and kodak.com/go/followus.

Our social media strategy

At Kodak we focus on using social media as an additional channel to amplify our messages, to increase product awareness and to have a direct dialogue with our customers. We created individual social media channels in nine European countries to engage with the consumers in their local language on their preferred channels and make it easy for them to reach us. We work on establishing lasting relationships with our customers that go beyond specific product launches. We give them a voice in our product development and turn them into brand ambassadors. Through our social media activities we want to help people to easily discover, recommend, select, purchase and use our products and services, wherever they are in the world. Our primary objectives are to positively impact demand generation activities across multiple channels, improve the Kodak customer experience and connection, and accelerate the pace and quality of feedback for our marketing and product plans.

On the commercial side, it is about providing thought leadership to the industries we serve. By showcasing the expertise at Kodak we can help our customers navigate changes in technology. We make connections with peers and provide answers to questions they may have about our products and services and the industry as a whole. We want to be a trusted source of relevant information and provide valuable insights and advice on issues our customers and partners care about. We have established individual social media channels for our business-to-business (B2B) customers and peers, to meet the interest of this specific audience. We also created and engage in a generic LinkedIn group called "PrintZone" where we talk specifically with business users about their markets and interests, and discuss how we can make our products better suited to them. To make our B2B social media contest easily accessible, we created a so-called Social Media Newsroom www.kodak.com/go/KodakB2B that shows the latest posts from the various channels in real-time on one page.

To ensure we have enough valuable content for our social media channels we have created, and are constantly growing, an internal team of active contributors to our Kodak social media marketing activities including video, blog posts, webinars, tweets as well as attendance at events, shows and conferences.

You can get an overview of all Kodak social media channels on our follow us pages www.kodak.com/go/followus.

A recent social media success story

Background

We recognize that the B2B buying process has fundamentally changed. Today buyers are moving into the sales funnel much later than ever before. Prospects are spending more time on the web doing research, connecting with their peers and third-party influencers via social media. They are relying on content found on social media channels to educate themselves about products and services. So, in 2010, we started focusing on using our Kodak events and activities for content creation as well as real time sharing and engagement with our B2B audience via social media.

We used social media extensively when we participated at IPEX trade show in Birmingham in 2010, and the lessons we learned from this have been rolled out globally.

Campaign objective

- To drive users to Kodak content online during IPEX and increase brand awareness.
- To drive visitors to the Kodak booth and the K-Zone panel discussions, and increase our follower base and brand impressions on our social media channels.
- To maximize the trade show investment by increasing engagement with our peers, educate prospects, both at the show and beyond via online channels.
- To attract third-party influencers and increase traffic across our blogs and online channels.

Our main goals were to create further awareness of our products and services, to drive leads while establishing Kodak as a leader in B2B social media, to add value to the conversation, to build a brand personality and to highlight the people behind the products.

Budget

This activation campaign was part of the IPEX trade show marketing and communications budget. It included two social media experts as dedicated resources in a blogging zone at the trade show to implement the social media activation.

What we did

At IPEX 2010 in Birmingham we set up a "K-Zone" for the very first time at a European trade show. The K-Zone is a show within a show, where a series of sessions with unscripted panels happen on the latest trends in the graphic arts and about how to optimize your business. Each panel consists of well-known industry experts, influencers and print professionals. It is a forum to learn and share from the experiences of others. The IPEX K-Zone sessions were broadcast live over the internet and the videos were posted online.

This was enhanced by an IPEX "blogging zone" where Jennifer Cisney, Kodak Chief Blogger, and myself, shared all activities at the Kodak booth as well as the content and learnings from the K-Zone via Twitter, Facebook, YouTube and our Kodak blogs. That way people around the world could participate in real time.

ROI

We used Radian6 to measure reach, participation, impact and influence of our social media activities at IPEX 2010. The results showed that we achieved 60 per cent share of voice online during the whole IPEX trade show week. This meant businesses around the world were talking more about Kodak at IPEX than they were about our competitors and their products.

Kodak emerged from IPEX 2010 as a B2B social media leader with specific mentions of our technology, our products, our marketing and our social media efforts.

Key learnings

- The majority of IPEX conversations occurred on Twitter (80 per cent).
- Blogs (13.9 per cent)+mainstream media and forums (5.5 per cent) made up the remaining volume.
- During the first half of the show the Kodak K-Zone and other Kodak topics maintained a notable presence in all conversations online.

The trade show environment was the perfect platform for positioning Kodak B2B social media. We achieved all that we set out to.

Madlen's best advice

I strongly believe that businesses today benefit from direct interaction with both existing and potential customers in the social space. However, it is important that companies listen first and understand where their customers are online and what their needs are before engaging with them. When engaging in conversations, it is essential to "be real" and to connect in a transparent manner and only when value can be added to the conversation.

Another important point is to define your social media strategy then identify your goals and measures before "jumping in".

Want more? See what has been said about this case or get involved and discuss it with the author and other readers on our LinkedIn group, find it by visiting http://www.socialmedia-mba.com or search for "The Social Media MBA Alumni".

Chapter 18

Hans Notenboom, Global Director B2B Online

The author

Hans has over 20 years of experience in online marketing, new media and IT. He worked for many big brands developing online experiences and building communities. Hans is now globally responsible for social media, online marketing, CRM and internet analytics for Philips B2B businesses.

Twitter: @hansnotenboom

The company

Royal Philips Electronics of the Netherlands (NYSE: PHG, AEX: PHI) is a diversified health and well-being company, focused on improving people's lives through timely innovations. As a world leader in healthcare, lifestyle and lighting, Philips integrates technologies and design into people-centric solutions, based on fundamental customer insights and the brand promise of "sense and simplicity".

Headquartered in the Netherlands, Philips employs about 117,000 employees with sales and services in more than 100 countries worldwide. With sales of EUR 22.3 billion in 2010, the company is a market leader in cardiac care, acute care and home healthcare, energy efficient lighting solutions and new lighting applications, as well as lifestyle products for personal well-being and pleasure with strong leadership positions in male shaving and grooming, portable entertainment and oral healthcare.

Our social media strategy

The objective of our B2B social media strategy is to connect and drive thought leadership with our key audiences in healthcare and lighting. Historically, Philips knows it's difficult to build communities on our own platforms with these professionals. It's not only expensive to recruit these audiences and get enough insight in their profile, it also takes a lot of effort to keep the relationship and dialogue ongoing and data are quickly outdated.

The strategy of Philips is to go where the audience is already present and facilitate the discussion there. It has to be very easy to join our groups and participate. Philips abandoned the common principle of wanting to own email addresses. Using an available platform is much more viable. The strategic goal is to make the groups leading in their industry and self-sustainable.

LinkedIn proved the most interesting platform because large numbers of the right professionals are already registered and easy to recruit. LinkedIn, although historically most dominant in English speaking markets, is quickly growing and is also the biggest or most promising platform for B2B in almost all markets in the world, with over 100 million members.

Due to the nature of LinkedIn as a professional platform, we found that the level of engagement was deeper and more sustained with the members that joined the groups. With each comment linked to that member's professional identity, the discussions were of a higher quality than we might have seen on a social network or blog, for example. This also helped other members see who was sharing insights, which creates a much more valuable experience.

Strong integration with Twitter, other Philips owned or sponsored platforms and our own internet site completes a seamless experience. On LinkedIn, Philips is facilitating discussion of trends and industry issues. For discussions on Philips products, support or business opportunities, we refer the members to Philips' own domains.

Philips allocated a substantial startup budget to the partnership with LinkedIn to get access to the platform with featured groups, additional support and enough recruitment and advertising in LinkedIn to get the groups going. The groups are moderated by Philips in cooperation with OneVoice, their PR agency. Philips staff members are actively participating in the groups as hosts and contributors or subject matter experts.

The groups are originally setup by global marketing, currently handed over to the business sectors. Marketers in the sector can now leverage the platform to learn, engage in discussion or participate.

Recent social media success story

Background

In mid 2010 a strategic partnership was established with LinkedIn. In a very short period of time the groups were set up, enriched with relevant content and functionalities, Philips hosts were trained and moderation organized. Based on a clear definition of the target audience, the recruitment started. In a period of six to seven months the key objectives were already achieved and various subgroups on specialty topics were launched.

Campaign objective

Based on research, Philips concluded that a group of at least 15,000 relevant members is a lively and self-sustainable group. Within six months these targets were reached. The healthcare group reached the top three position worldwide and the lighting group the number one position based on member base. This delivers extra traffic and the group is now self-sustainable. More than 99 per cent of the discussions are started by members. Another objective is to attract the right audience. Based on the LinkedIn profile this can be measured very specifically. The biggest groups of members are exactly the desired target like the clinical staff in healthcare and the architects and specifiers in lighting.

Secondly, the objective is to drive thought leadership. Throughout the company, Philips measured how customers perceive us through Net Promoter Score (NPS) measurement. The groups need to show that they create more promoters.

Budget

The startup budget for the programme was almost completely allocated to the recruitment of the desired audience and a small portion of moderation. Now that the groups are large and self-sustainable the growth is through the professional network of the members and the top position in LinkedIn, resulting in a much lower recruitment need. On the other hand, the large member base requires more attention for moderation.

Delivery

A small social media team was established in global marketing to drive the initiative. Due to the extensive support from LinkedIn, the Philips team could focus on organizing the moderation and the internal foundation. The team recruited internal hosts and subject matter experts. The project was managed through a weekly team meeting with LinkedIn and the moderation partner and a quarterly extended meeting.

LinkedIn worked closely with us to define our target audience and help us quickly narrow down from 100 million members to the exact professionals we wanted to reach. We were able to target members by job title, function, seniority, company, industry, location, keywords and other facets to make sure the promotion of the groups was efficient.

ROI

On a monthly base an extensive report is delivered with all key metrics including members, member profiles, engagement, insights generated and NPS scores. All groups have shown very positive NPS scores. The engagement with members stays high, compared to other large professional groups. Every now and then members indicate a commercial interest. It's not the prime objective of the group, but of course these requests are followed up. Last but not least, the group is generating insights used in product development, marketing and sales, for instance going deep into the best usage of MRI scanners.

Hans' best advice

The most important lesson for Philips is that we can build a relationship with prime audiences without owning the relationship itself. It's more practical and successful to go where your audience is as opposed to trying to create a new community from scratch. Other key points are:

- keep it simple; and
- be open and transparent.

For instance competitors are free to join the community as long as they follow the rules. One purpose of the moderation is to keep the group clean of spam and job-hunters and interesting to the audience. Having trusted hosts and experts, and empowering internal staff to participate, makes the group even more relevant. It's a great way for an organization to listen to customers and learn.

> Want more? See what has been said about this case or get involved and discuss it with the author and other readers on our LinkedIn group, find it by visiting http://www.socialmedia-mba.com or search for "The Social Media MBA Alumni".

Chapter 19

Cath Sheldon, Online PR Specialist

The author

Cath Sheldon joined Sage in 2007 as a web copywriter. She then worked as Digital Campaign Manager before her current role as Online PR Specialist, in which Cath has been responsible for driving Sage's social media strategy and the content of the Sage blog and Twitter feed (@sageuk).

The company

Sage (UK) Limited is a subsidiary of The Sage Group plc, a leading global supplier of business management software solutions and related products and services.

In the UK, Sage is made up of four divisions: Sage Pay, Small Business, Mid Market and Accountants Division. It provides software and services to more than 800,000 businesses ranging from startups to FTSE 100 companies. This software ranges from accounts and ERP, HR and payroll, forecasting and business intelligence to customer relationship management, e-business and help for startups. Services include Excel support, HR advice, health and safety advice and training courses.

Sage employs more than 2,000 employees in the UK.

Our social media strategy

The overall objective for social media at Sage is to use it to keep its customers at the heart of the business. To achieve this, Sage ensured from the very start that it had the buy-in of both the customer service and marketing teams.

Once this was achieved Sage identified online influencers relevant to each of its divisions, monitored conversations about Sage and then started to engage with key stakeholders through its profiles across the different social media platforms. This method was used as a way to demonstrate Sage's extraordinary customer experience, as it is about more than just listening to conversations. It is about learning and applying what has been discovered to make a better experience.

The next phase involved the PR team creating and promoting content and embedding social media within all PR and marketing activities. This phase saw Sage focusing efforts on demonstrating its thought leadership on industry issues relevant to customers through the introduction of the Sage blog and by adding comments to relevant and influential discussion forums when appropriate.

Running alongside this activity was a strong internal engagement strategy, where employees were educated about Sage's social media strategy and empowered to support the company's social media activities.

Sage has a flexible PR policy that allows anyone from the company to become involved in representing Sage in social media. This is, however, coordinated by a central PR team who ensure that all activities are customer centric and meet the business objectives.

Social media has become a key channel for dialogue with customers and stakeholders for Sage. It has official profiles on Twitter, YouTube and the Sage blog and all content on these platforms must adhere to the guiding principle that it adds value to our customers.

Recent social media success story

Background

One area where Sage's social media activity has particularly excelled is the ongoing customer service delivered via Twitter. The company has organically grown its follower base to more than 6,000 people who regularly engage with the company. Sage's transparent approach has seen the company build customers' trust, as well as establish itself as an important channel for product and service development.

Campaign objective

Sage's objective was to enhance and protect the company's reputation online, but to also demonstrate its extraordinary customer experience.

Sage passionately believes that social media offers a fantastic opportunity to hear the voice of its customers, and the company uses the knowledge and insights it gains from engaging with customers to improve its services, products and the experience that it provides.

Delivery

Twitter was identified as providing a fantastic platform for user feedback on a real-time basis, which meant that any issues or trends impacting customers could be identified early, and by working with the relevant parts of the business, quickly resolved.

Sage initially used Twitter for customer insights, monitoring sentiment and collating feedback on particular products. However, it also provided the company with a greater visibility of its users and offered opportunities to interact directly with customers and prospects to ensure that the customer remained at the heart of all activity.

For an integrated marketing campaign, Sage used all of the social media platforms to connect with its customers and source best business tips and hints. Using the Sage blog as a central hub all entries were then collated and compiled into a practical guide to offer small businesses with advice. As well as people directly submitting tips via the blog, there was a lot of online buzz created on Twitter from people retweeting suggestions and promoting the competition running alongside the campaign.

ROI

As with all types of social media, it is very hard to put a monetary value on interaction and influence, so it was decided from the off that success would be measured by engagement levels.

For Twitter this was done by looking at the number of Twitter followers; their influence on Twitter; how many users visited the Sage blog from links posted from a tweet; and the average time spent on the Sage web site. It was evident, when the data from these factors were collected, that the Sage Twitter feed has been a hugely successful platform for interaction.

For the integrated marketing campaign success came in the number of people who downloaded the guide, which on last count was more than 2,500. Not only was this activity a nice collaborative effort, where Sage's customers had the chance to share their expertise with other customers, but it also enabled the company to develop an insightful piece of content.

Key learnings

- Brands should embrace social media and give it a go. There is no one size fits all, but if companies start small and learn as they go, it will be possible to find what works and what should be left to other firms.
- Social media is a vast platform that is always changing. It's vital that internally within a company there is a continuous flow of information regarding activity plans, progress and success stories. It is so important to have buy-in from your colleagues from the start as it will ensure that the interaction and updates are in keeping with other activities and that the brand continues to have a unified voice.
- Ensure that social media is integrated at the planning stages of campaigns, so that there is the opportunity to make suggestions and test ideas out before it is too late and people expect results.

- It is imperative at the early stages, but should be maintained throughout, to track, report back and prove ROI on all social media activity. This will not only build trust within the company but will also allow you to see what has worked well and how activity can be refined for the next campaign.

Cath's best advice

It is vital that before you start any social media activity you have clear objectives and a strategy in place. It is easy otherwise to become distracted by the social media noise and lose sight of what your aim was.

Want more? See what has been said about this case or get involved and discuss it with the author and other readers on our LinkedIn group, find it by visiting http://www.socialmedia-mba.com or search for "The Social Media MBA Alumni".

Part V

The Future

Chapter 20

Why one size does not fit all in the world
of digital communications

Michael Netzley

In short

- Why Western companies must respond to local needs in Asia if they wish to grow.
- How to best embrace the opportunities in these markets.
- What you have to gain by breaking the mould others are stuck in.

Overview

In this chapter Michael Netzley, PhD at the Singapore Management University, discusses the opportunity to see beyond the traditional markets. Asia is filled with diverse and fragmented markets, more so than what we typically find in the West's more mature markets. The larger social media conversation reflects values and market assumptions of these mature markets, and all too often the needs of Asia's emerging and growing markets go unrepresented. Professional communicators must stop relying on advice crafted within different market conditions and instead lead the way forward by producing solid research as the basis for data-driven communication decisions.

The tsunami is washing across northern Japan and my television screen as I write my thoughts regarding biases in our digital media conversation. The terrible tragedy taking place in a country that I briefly called home appears on a scale I have not seen since the Aceh tsunami in 2004. Images of the destruction flow across my screen, and as commentators worry about the nation's nuclear power plants I am equally taken by the immediate outpouring of sympathy for the people of Japan. The pace of tweets in the #Japan column of Tweetdeck seems to be accelerating with each hour as the world wakes to this tragedy. Like many, I share my thoughts of sympathy via social media.

For the time being, the world's attention is rightly focused on Asia.

But, like all news cycles, with time other stories will press to the forefront of public attention and the efforts at rebuilding in Japan will slowly move to page two, then section b and so on. Such is the ethos of global media – mainstream and digital – in a world oversaturated with stories.

While unquestionably a tragedy, what do the events in Japan have to do with digital media in Asia? My answer is "a lot."

Sitting in the comforts of Singapore, where I have taught a university-level course in digital media since 2007, my personal assessment is that the pattern of attention I attribute to Japan is little different than the global pattern of our social media conversation (as we like to call it). When significant events attract enough attention, such as Google threatening to leave China or Facebook's Mark Zuckerberg taking a trip to China, the digital community turns its attention east. But with time, discussion and speculation give way to other news stories and Asia disappears from the social media centre stage.

The bulk of what we crowdsource, curate and speculate about digital media comes from outside Asia. Yet, Asia currently makes up the world's largest segment (in terms of total numbers) of the world's internet population and includes some of its fastest growing markets at the start of 2011. But for a complex suite of reasons, the centre of gravity regarding our discussion of everything digital seems to be found in the West. What we know about digital media and communications is, in my assessment, comparatively limited. Even from an academic perspective, most of the research in public relations, marketing and corporate reputation come from the West and are based on results in those markets. Why should social media be any different?

We have, I believe, an ethnocentric bias in our discussion of digital communications.

So what is an ethnocentric bias? This bias can be thought of as a "dire need for multiculturalism" in how we discuss communications (Sriramesh, 2002). I argue that the cultural attributes underpinning the broader discussion of integration into business, politics and society reflect the biases of North America and Western Europe. Consider this simple example: how many people in 2011 continue to ask if the internet can serve as a democratic force capable of unseating authoritarian governments? As an American I have much in common with this question, but as an expat living in Asia for nearly a decade, I also see the question as rather idealistic.

"And so what?", some readers may ask. A fair question indeed, and in response I would point out many of the global changes that we are all well aware of. Economic and soft power shifts eastward as countries like China, India and Indonesia improve their social and economic conditions while Western economies appear anaemic under crushing debt. Numerous business and news reports have discussed the BRIC economies, now sometimes referred as the BRICI economies with the inclusion of Indonesia, and their increasing importance. The growing middle classes in many Asian countries are now consumers who buy Western goods, pay full tuition for their kids to attend Western universities and now carry the pride and confidence of people coming into their own. Looking at digital markets, we also see that many of the fastest-growing internet markets are found in Asia. From South Korea to Singapore, China to Indonesia, and India to Australia there can be little doubt that global power shifts are underway. The diversity and complexity of markets demands that we do not look at digital media through a one size fits most lens. As professional communicators, we will increasingly find ourselves engaging Asia in a multitude of ways.

> The diversity and complexity of markets demands that we do not look at digital media through a one size fits most lens.

Key characteristics of the current discussion

Before proceeding further, I need to be a bit more specific about this thing I call the "discussion." As a voracious consumer of web sites, reports, podcasts and books devoted to digital media, allow me to begin by looking at precisely this content we all encounter each day. We can begin with the world's most visited web destinations (Alexa, 2011).

1. Google
2. Facebook
3. YouTube
4. Yahoo
5. Windows Live
6. Blogger
7. Baidu
8. Wikipedia
9. Twitter
10. QQ.com

Two of the top ten destinations are from outside North America and in Asia to be specific. Baidu and QQ are located in China, the world's largest internet market. Looking a bit more broadly at the top 20, sites such as Yahoo Japan, Sina.com.cn and Google India appear. The top global destinations are largely Western, a few are Western businesses with local offices, and only about 15 per cent of the top 20 sites are businesses created outside the West.

It seems perfectly normal that we prefer to talk about what is biggest or most popular. And in Asian markets we seek out any sign that we are somehow a part of this global trend. We want to see ourselves as, and be seen as, part of something that is taking the world by storm. So, in March, when it was announced that Jakarta was the world's Facebook capital, people around the region (including Indonesians) gave out a collective victory cry (Socialbakers, 2011a).

Western social media sites, case studies and discussions also seem to command the overwhelming share of voice in top selling books. I next looked at social media books sold via Amazon.com. My goal here is not, in any way, to criticize these best-selling books, the authors or the content. In fact, I purchased, read and enjoyed many of these titles. I want only to illustrate the pattern I am seeing in terms of content and perspective shared.

A quick look at Amazon.com's top 100 books in March 2011, listed under a "social media" search for relevance, revealed that only three of the top 100 books explicitly identify Asia as a region worth a book, chapter or even prominent case study. These books instead were dominated by the most popular topics that you might expect (including but not limited to): Zappos, Coca Cola, Starbucks, Ford, Google, Huffington Post, Dell, Digg, Google, Yahoo and Craigslist.

I next visited the Ad Age Power 150 daily ranking of marketing blogs and sought out top blogs focusing on Asia in any noticeable way. Immediately, just by glancing at the flags showing the nationality of the top blogs, only one out of the 150 blogs claimed a nationality outside of North America or Western Europe (Ad Age, 2011). Further investigation into that one blog revealed no obvious focus on markets other than the West. The top 50 blogs revealed exactly the same pattern (Technorati, 2011). In terms of the blogosphere, both authors and content appear to be shaped with a Western-centric point of view. The topics in the blogs were little different than the books I examined.

The one little bit of good news came when I turned to the academic research being published about social media use in higher education. Asia gets a bit more recognition when we turn to scholarly, peer-reviewed research published in journals. Limiting myself to academic research published in 2010 and accessed through the university library database Science Direct, I identified 97 scholarly articles with the key words *blogs*, *wikis* or *mobile*, which reported scholarly research study findings from around the world. The studies, when grouped geographically based on where the participant sample population came from, had the following breakdown: 70.1 per cent came from Western cultures in North America, all of Europe, Australia and New Zealand; 25.7 per cent from greater Asia; and the remaining articles from Latin America, Middle East and Africa.

But as I turned from the academic to commercially produced reports, Asia quickly falls off the radar screen. To be fair, several very good commercial reports, which included Asian markets, were published in 2010. Nielsen, Yahoo-Synovate "Net Index", KPMG's "Consumers and Convergence", TNS "Global Digital Life", Burson Marsteller's Corporate Social Media Report, Edelman's "Trust Barometer" and "Digital Brand Index", Boston Consulting Group's "The Internet's New Billion", Universal McCann's "Wave" report, ComScore's report on South East Asia, and a variety of releases from the Asia Digital Marketing Association dominate Asia's commercial report landscape (ComScore, 2011). Two points, however, stand out.

First, many of these reports look at China, India or Japan, as their sample population. As you will see shortly, Asia is composed of many fragmented markets with different platform preferences and online behaviours. No one or two countries could possibly represent the entire region. There is no single Asia.

Second, perhaps with the exception of the Yahoo-Synovate Net Index studies, few commercial businesses look at the ASEAN markets. In all fairness, this could possibly happen because of limited opportunities to recoup any investments made into these mostly emerging markets. But in the case of Singapore, which is a very advanced economy, market size might be an issue. With a market of only 5 million people and an average household income in 2011 of SG$5,000 per month, again the market opportunity may simply be too small.

Solid research findings based on a suitable sample size and reliable instrument are scarce, and there is a serious shortage of reliable data about many Asian markets.

Any claim about an ethnocentric bias would be remiss without also considering the nature of many Asian markets and the businesses operating within. Many of Asia's leading internet businesses likely appear foreign to much of the world because they were designed with the local tastes in mind. Baidu and QQ in China, Mixi and Gree in Japan, and Cyworld and Naver in South Korea are the classic examples.

One of the key reasons why these local sites have such a strong advantage over the global competitors like Facebook and Google, and in some cases soundly defeated them, is sociolinguistic differences. Not only do internet users in China, South Korea, Japan, Indonesia, Thailand and India (to name a few) typically not speak Western languages at home, but they also have different social expectations and behave quite differently online. So when consumers choose between a local platform that feels like a natural fit, and a foreign competitor that seems less intuitive, the local businesses often triumph.

When we mix it all together, a complex set of reasons emerge for what I see as the dominance of Western voices and topics in the social media discussion. At the most basic level, there are more people around the world using and talking about, for example, Facebook than Cyworld. This statement is in no way a criticism, but a simple fact. However, beyond that, looking at the most popular sites, successful books, academic research and commercial research, I see North America and Europe holding an overwhelming share of voice.

Unfortunately, the conversation as I have described it here seems difficult to reconcile, in some respects, with the market size and user activity we see in Asia.

Asia's social media scene

Forecasts of the world's internet population in Figure 20.1 show that an increasing portion of users will come from Asia.

Asia, however, is not a homogenous region by any stretch of the imagination. It is home to more than 2,000 spoken languages, political models ranging from monarchies to democracies to authoritarian governments, incredible wealth and unforgiving poverty, and numerous religions. And when it comes to social media, there is a common expression, which goes something like this.

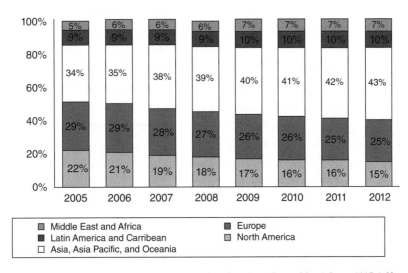

Source: Jupiter Research Worldwide Internet Population Model (3/08)   Steven Noble, Senior Analyst, Forrester Research. Presented Ad-Tech, SG

Figure 20.1: Asia: tapping into the trend

South Korea has one of the world's most advanced information societies, Japan has the world's most advanced mobile market, and China has the world's largest internet market which functions like a giant technology incubator.

At this point we could draw from a host of additional statistics to illustrate the amazing digital activity in Asia. These statistics, at the start of 2011, include the following:

- China Internet Watch (2011) reported that the number of internet users in the Mainland of China had reached 457 million by 2011 (projected to reach 500 million by mid-year). North America has 266 million internet users.
- Indonesia is currently the second largest Facebook community in the world with 35 million users out of a total internet user population of only 40 million people out of a total country population of 240 million (Socialbakers, 2011b).
- South Korea is the world's number two information society as reported by the International Telecommunications Union.
- User behaviours vary significantly from country to country. The Chinese show an appetite for the old fashioned bulletin board systems and active online engagement while, in contrast, Singaporeans are generally reserved online and consume content without engaging. Australians, according to the data, seem to be heavy social networkers.

Social media is in Asia, and in a big way.

So I hope that now the problem emerges more clearly. The social media conversation, in my view, is currently dominated by topics, case studies and advice out of North America and Western Europe. However, sitting in Singapore and studying the media markets across Asia, I observe markets that have limited similarity to the social media accounts I so commonly read. This disconnect, what I call ethnocentrism, is a problem for anyone trying to figure out how to succeed online with marketing, PR, sales or community building.

What works in the West will not transfer one-to-one in the East. Our efforts must be localized.

As a university professor, I am especially attuned to the relative lack of reliable research reports and case studies. I would be hard pressed to recall how many times I have been solicited, as a conference speaker or host, for more local cases. The pleas are that I make every effort to not have another speaker discuss the Old Spice campaign or Obama's election campaign. The same can be said of executive education participants, MBA class members and undergraduates – they all ask where are the local cases? They are tired of discussing another Google case study from Harvard (yet voraciously consume the latest news *about* Google). Many an audience has clapped after a speech, kindly complimented the speaker and exited the conference facilities expressing displeasure only to friends.

There is an audience in Asia hungry for local insights.

Leadership and the path forward

In an article titled "The Shift of PR Wealth to Asia" written by Burson-Marsteller's APAC President and CEO Bob Pickard (2011), important advice was shared with readers working in Asian markets.

> There is a long tradition of complaining about Western-centrism in Asia, with many derisive of those with 'global' titles who are thought to lack understanding of the Asian context. Sometimes these complaints seem valid but what we're going to find now with this shift of global PR power is that it's easy to criticise but a lot harder to paint on the bigger global communications canvases we're seeing on our side of the Pacific for the first time.

Simply put, are we going to sit back and complain or will we embrace and act on the opportunity these increasingly important markets are presenting to us? I am all for action, and considering the nature of these markets, fragmented and many of emerging-market status, I think a particular kind of leadership is required.

The answer, I believe, rests in public private partnerships (PPP). Markets are not the solution. If left to their own devices, for profit companies will only research markets within which they stand a reasonable chance of getting a return on their investment.

This raises two immediate concerns:

- What happens to small markets like Singapore and Brunei, or to still-developing markets like Thailand, Philippines and Pakistan?
- Market-driven solutions will likely limit the research scope to activities, which are in some sense billable or, in social media language, able to be monetized.

What about NGOs, governmental communications or the use of social media in education and developing the digital literacy of our children?

In Asia, many people look to the government for leadership and solutions. This notion of state solutions, while anathema in some places, can be openly embraced in parts of Asia Pacific. This point offers one more – poignant – example of just how different the East can be. And now, my call for PPP falls into alignment with the ideas presented earlier in this chapter. There is a critical role for governments, businesses and academics to play. The needs are broad, and the ability to learn from these diverse vantage points is great.

What I am describing is a leadership challenge that is harmonious in its balance of public interest and the profit motive. Any Western company or individual pursuing this challenge will need to display strong leadership in balancing the competing needs and, above all else, function as a learning organization. With fragmented markets, different stages of market maturity, global competition, diverse cultures and regulatory uncertainty in some cases, bridging the different needs will not be easy.

But, then again, it is precisely this sort of challenge that ultimately led many professionals to make Asia their home and to rise each morning to face these challenges, which never fail to excite, distress and compel each of us.

Roundup

> Want more? See what has been said about this chapter or get involved and discuss it with the author and other readers on our LinkedIn group, find it by visiting http://www.socialmedia-mba.com or search for "The Social Media MBA Alumni".

Days after the tragedy in Japan in 2011 we saw the best of what people using social media have to offer. Examples included online mapping projects, sharing stories that needed to be told, sourcing for resources and donations, and updating news reports and warnings around the nuclear plants.

This is leadership, and I think all businesses wanting to operate anywhere in Asia will benefit from taking a leaf or two from this book. We can see how online activities are localized and use similar yet tailored approaches to better communicate and make positive changes in all walks of life. One size does not fit all in Asia.

In the absence of reliable data about your market, competitors' communications or customers, what are three practical steps for researching your target audience and making data driven decisions about your communications? Start by being specific about the data you want and how you would get it. Then, allow the market-specific data to guide your decision making.

In the next chapter Zaheer Nooruddin will continue to paint the picture of the social media opportunity in Asia.

References

Ad Age (2011) Power 150. Retrieved on 13 March 13 2011 from http://adage.com/power150/.

Alexa (2011) Top sites. Retrieved from http://www.alexa.com/topsites.

China Internet Watch (2011) China Internet users by the numbers February 2011. Retrieved from http://www.facebook.com/notes/china-internet-watch/china -internet-users-by-numbers-feb-2011/496984821166.

Comscore (2011) State of the Internet with a Focus on SE Asia. Retrieved from http://www.comscore.com/Press_Events/Presentations_Whitepapers/2010/State_of_the_Internet_with_a_focus_on_Asia_Pacific.

Jupiter Research (2008) Wordwide online population forecast, 2007–2012. Retrieved from http://www.marketresearch.com/product/display.asp?productid=1900875.

Pickard, B. (2011) The shift of PR wealth to Asia. Holmes Report, retrieved from http://www.holmesreport.com/thinktank-info/10544/The-shift-of-PR-wealth-to-Asia.aspx.

Socialbakers (2011a) Socialbakers launches Facebook city statistics! Retrieved from http://www.socialbakers.com/blog/129-socialbakers-launches-Facebook-city-statistics/.

Socialbakers (2011b) Indonesia Facebook statistics. Retrieved from http://www.socialbakers.com/Facebook-statistics/indonesia.

Sriramesh, K. (2002) The dire need for multiculturalism in PR education: An Asian perspective. *Journal of Communication Management* 7(1), 54–70.

Technorati (2011) Top 100. Retrieved from http://technorati.com/blogs/top100.

Chapter 21

A brief history of social media in Asia and what businesses need to know

Zaheer Nooruddin

In short

- Why microblogging in China is such a unique story.
- How different Asian markets vary.
- What is the extent of social media use in Asia?

Overview

In this chapter, Zaheer Nooruddin, Digital Chief Marketing Officer and Lead Digital Strategist at Burson-Marsteller Asia-Pacific based in Hong Kong, will introduce you to the dynamic and diverse social media landscapes of the Asian continent. He will examine the most compelling reasons for businesses to participate in social media, the opportunities for communications and marketing, while understanding the many challenges they will face in Asia. He will invite you to consider how companies and organizations doing business in Asia should think to incorporate social media and digital storytelling into their integrated communications and marketing strategies in Asian markets.

Here's an amazing fact for you to consider: by 2012, the Asian continent will account for half of all internet users worldwide.

Now consider this: just China by itself already produces more than half the world's internet content, and more than the rest of the world combined.

Living, in Asia, as I do, one can't help but be fascinated by the sheer numbers one hears about the internet and social media in this part of the world. Encompassing mammoth nations like China and India, the growth story of Asia has only just begun. Indeed, as far as the internet goes, this century is Asia's century – and the future is Asia's.

Let's begin with China: with 1 billion 4 hundred million citizens, 460 million of which were PC internet users at the beginning of 2011 and an ongoing increase to that number of 10 million users per month, there is no other market that can come close to competing in the numbers game.

But China is just one country in Asia, and it is just a chapter in the Asian internet story. With over half of the world's population spread across 35 diverse countries and vast regions – spreading from the northern latitudes of the Korean peninsula all the way to New Zealand in the far southern reaches – the vast and teeming continent of Asia is the world's largest and most populous.

How, you ask, can a continent with less than half of the world's internet users be considered the "future of the internet"? The answer lies in the numbers. Nowhere else on Earth is the number of internet users growing as rapidly, year on year, as in Asia. With a 620 per cent user average growth rate between the years 2000 and 2010, compared to 360 per cent in the rest of the world – almost half of Asia's growth – there is no other region in the world that is growing so rapidly, and more importantly, with so much more potential for growth in the future.

While the story of the early worldwide web, the web 2.0 and social media innovation, was written in the Western world, the "Far East" is beginning to play a significant part in shaping – and in some cases, even leading – innovation in the new global social media landscape.

Even as I write this, China's most popular, home-grown Twitter-like microblogging service from Sina, one of the nation's internet technology powerhouses, is preparing to release an English version of its "weibo" ("micro-blogging" to the Chinese) platform.

Many analysts have speculated that Sina Weibo (weibo.com) is already ahead of Twitter in its services and features, rapidly outpacing its competitors by innovating and rolling out new, integrated social networking features (that make it more Facebook-like – or even, dare I say, more Google+-like – every time it does so) and offering its API to other platforms, to developers and consumers.

Today more web and mobile apps are being developed in Asia, and Asian social media adoption rates will soon overtake the Western world. Asia's social media entrepreneurs are waging a quiet battle, getting ready to storm the world with their awesome technologies.

Even though internet penetration in China still hovers around 25 per cent – what seems like a modest figure – the country has the world's largest internet population already, surpassing the USA by far, and approaching 500 million users by the beginning of 2012.

Nielsen CR reported that, as of December 2009, China had already reached 221 million bloggers, more than twice the number in the US.

Back to Asia – there is one other critical point in the continent's amazing internet growth story that should not be ignored – and that is the reach of mobile devices. We are witnessing a profoundly interesting time in Asia in 2012 – as most Asian markets evolve their telecommunications systems from 2G to 3G networking. This seminal shift in connectivity, combined with the rise of Smartphones that are becoming rapidly more affordable, every year for the rest of this decade, is creating a tectonic shift in online usage in Asia's emerging economies and societies – one that is set to make the rest of the developed world stand up and take notice.

Gone are the days when Smartphones and tablets were the domain of the well-heeled. Today, with cheap mobile device handsets becoming available and the proliferation of Android and other open system operating technologies, the market is wide open, and nowhere more so than in Asia (see Figure 21.1).

The convergence of rapidly evolving mobile handset and operating system technologies, faster telecommunications and affordable price point, make for a dynamic mobile web landscape. And companies all across Asia are beginning to pay attention to this critical shift in consumer behaviour.

In China, for example, there are credible projections that indicate there will be as many as 800 million mobile Smartphone users by 2015.

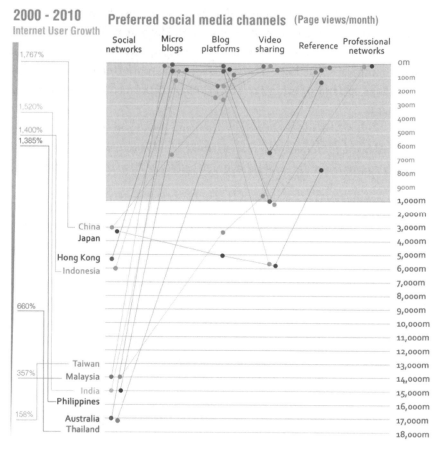

Figure 21.1: Internet user growth in Asia
Source: Zaheer Nooruddin. Used with his kind permission.

That's in a mere four years. Think long and hard about that number: 800 million.

In India – a large country that suffers from infrastructural issues like perhaps no other – there are already 500 million users of mobile phones. As the average Indian gets slightly more prosperous, and the cost of mobile devices reduces each year – particularly smart and feature phones that allow internet access – vast numbers of mobile users will turn into mobile internet users. Of course, the number of Indians who own mobile devices is also increasing exponentially each year. So the next few years could see as many as a billion Indians connected to the internet directly via their mobile devices, doing a leap-frog right past internet usage numbers in many of the European nations combined.

The same story – although in more digestible numbers – can be seen right across Asia, from Pakistan to Sri Lanka to Vietnam.

Today, a staggering 98 per cent of internet users in the Philippines are actively using Facebook. Twitter is another international platform that is enjoying a strong resurgence in Asia due to its iPhone, Android, Windows and iPad apps that make it accessible on mobile devices. Indonesia, for example, has seen strong growth in microblogging as a social media channel and it today claims the top spot in terms of Twitter users as a proportion of total internet users. The Philippines and Singapore have also recently joined Indonesia in the list of countries around the world with the highest reach into Twitter, ranked at numbers six and nine respectively.

While there might soon be more users of Twitter in Indonesia than perhaps in any other country in the world, in Japan, Korea, Australia, New Zealand, Singapore and Hong Kong total internet penetrations among these markets' populations have already peaked at "saturation" levels – meaning that everyone is plugged in. From young to old, from rich to poor, from white collar to blue collar – in some form or another, everyone.

I shall never forget the time I called a plumber to fix a leak in my apartment in Hong Kong. He arrived, not with a toolkit as one would have expected, but to my amazement and slight annoyance, with an iPad and an iPhone in hand.

The absolute triumph of social media in Asia

In Asia, over the next decade, two trends are crystal clear. The first: further, massive internet penetration in just about every developing Asian country. The second: a rising sense of prosperity for people throughout the region.

As incredibly diverse as the Pan-Asian continent is – and it is – one thing can be said of all Asians: they are by and large a gregarious and sociable people. They love to share.

Perhaps sharing is, above all, just a dominant human trait.

In Asia, online sharing takes place in a bewildering variety of places, collectively representing the diverse landscape of social media. Some of Asia's biggest markets have evolved their own unique social network services distinct from those of Europe and North America. However, the situation is not simple to analyse. International social platforms and applications that traditionally performed better in more Westernized Asian markets such as Australia and Singapore have strong local competition is some Asian markets.

In many parts of Asia, as can be seen in Figure 21.2, the most popular international social media and networking platforms have yet to extend their dominance, where local social platforms still hold sway. Nowhere is this truer than in China, where entrenched local social networks enjoy a dominant position in that vast and lucrative market.

Although the battle for consumer share of time is waged fiercely between a myriad of local platforms, ranging from microblogging services to full-blown social networks to specialist online bulletin boards, local players enjoy a unique position of having international competitors shut out from the game. The "Great Firewall" of China, enabled and policed by the Chinese government to maintain "social order and harmony", has proved impenetrable for even the most influential and popular players elsewhere.

In China, there is no Facebook, no Twitter and no YouTube. For a time, there was no BBC and no Google Video. Unless one has a VPN (virtual private network) that allows access over the

> In China, there is no Facebook, no Twitter and no YouTube.

Great Firewall, one is constrained to the information and experiences inside of it. These are dominated by large local players, offering a mixed bag of services and social features.

Central to social media in China is the bulletin board (BBS), a version of the online chat room that is now antiquated in Western markets, relegated to the nether regions of the social web. There are hundreds of thousands of BBS platforms in China, each offering conversations around distinct topics, with followers from different parts of its geography, divided and united mainly by interest and proximity.

All around Asia, as internet penetration expands through broadband and mobile, social media has become "the connector" of communities. In the age

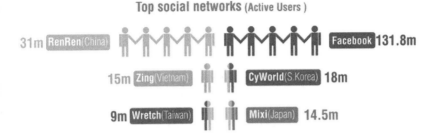

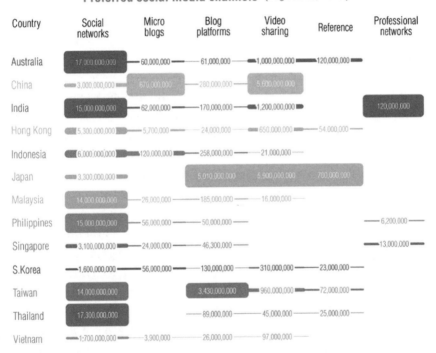

Figure 21.2: Most popular social networks and social media channels in Asia
Source: Zaheer Nooruddin. Used with his kind permission.

of social media, the prospering people of Asia, from Vietnam to India to Malaysia, enjoy a vast universe of social experiences online – from blogging to microblogging services, to video sharing, to social networking and online forums – all, quite literally, at their fingertips.

In a sense, therefore, social media and networking is not an "opt-in" choice for Asian users of the internet who are being plugged into the online experience during this decade – it is in the very DNA of online experiential adoption and web usage.

The unique story of microblogging in China

A report was published recently in the *Wall Street Journal*'s China Real Time Report, about how government authorities and agencies in China – of varying influence and nature – have embraced Sina's Weibo microblogging service. Weibo, as all China net watchers know, is a service that has caught on like wildfire in 2010, with over 50 million users by October, and a projected 150 million expected to join up by the end of 2011.

Sanctioned as the "de facto" microblogging service in China (China's Twitter, if you will) by the powers-that-be, and provided with all the necessary licenses to operate and take-off commercially in a big way, Sina's Weibo, with its unique features and characteristics, has caught the imagination of China's youth segment. The service is used to socialize, meet people, as a dating channel and for more serious pastimes as well, like spreading information about issues that are important to the Chinese people at large.

Companies and private enterprises too have been quick to catch onto the trend, and many have already adopted Weibo presences, to communicate in real-time with their audiences, and sometimes even to engage.

Interestingly, many international personalities and celebrities that are bent on influencing the Chinese public at large, such as Bill Gates (we all know who he is), Rio Ferdinand (the Manchester United/England team footballer) and Sora Aoi (the Japanese AV star), have also adopted Sina Weibo accounts of their own. They are therefore better at engaging than others – as is the case with Aoi, who has more than a million Chinese fans following her tweets. Aoi famously tweets on her own, responding to fans individually sometimes – making everyone involved very happy.

Which brings us to the Chinese authorities – who, not too long ago, were absolutely petrified of microblogging as a medium that could potentially be used by activists and dissidents to spread their messages around protest and societal injustice in real-time, and as a tool to organize and rally the public around anti-government issues. The reaction to microblogging then (circa

2009) was to rapidly and in quick succession shut down a number of first-generation Chinese microblogging services. These included microblogging sites like QQ's Tao Tao, Fanfou and Jiwai, among others.

While some of these platforms re-emerged in various manifestations, none managed to pick up steam and become as "mass" as Sina Weibo has. Not even China's Sohu, a similarly massive web ecosystem, has managed to replicate the success of Sina. Sohu's (sohu.com) flagging microblog service is almost never in the news, while Sina's Weibo is almost never out of it these days.

Getting the "nod" from the Chinese government, who at some point early last year realized that they cannot repress the urge of their young, active netizens to microblog – a cheap and easy pastime, with a very low threshold of commitment to it, unlike blogging, and the chance to communicate and engage via byte-sized messaging widely, as opposed to social networks platforms in China where influence is restricted to just one's known Friend's group – has proven huge for Sina's Weibo needless to say.

The authorities have taken on the "let's join them" approach with Weibo – and thousands of accounts have been created to monitor the goings on of Weibo's quickly expanding community. This, coupled with Sina's government-enforced monitoring and report system around sensitive keywords and topics, and the Chinese peoples' penchant for self-censorship, keeps Sina's Weibo manageable for the government in China. Having the flock tweeting away to each other "in one basket" helps matters for the purpose of monitoring and regulation.

Here's another microblogging service that didn't make it in China: Twitter!

The incredible dominance of social gaming and online dating in Asia

In China, Japan and South Korea, the growth of social networking in the mainstream has been driven by the adoption of online gaming as a leading pastime for the young and middle-aged.

Let's not forget that Farmville, that most popular of online social games, was developed in China, first, before taking grip in other markets including

Europe and North America. Spending increasing amounts of time on the internet and connecting to the web increasingly through mobile devices pre-loaded with webcams, the Asian youth and white collar demographic are busier than ever in their work.

If you are travelling on the Beijing subway, as on any of the mass transit systems of other Asian cities such as Tokyo, Singapore and Hong Kong, besides the sheer pulsating energy of the crowds, what will strike you is how connected people are in a mobile world. It seems that every other person is listening to music, watching a video, posting an update or playing a game. With seamless connectivity to the broadband internet for the first time, as an ever firmer reality for Asians living across the continent, irrespective of market, this means that travelling time, as well as work time, can be used to share, to experience and to connect.

Online gaming is huge all across Asia – just as it remains a pervasive force in most markets around the world.

Another social media phenomenon in Asia is online dating. As Asians have become more prosperous through the rapid urbanization that their markets are witnessing, they have also become very busy. Working 60–80 hour weeks in Asia's urban centres, the young demographic of Asia has increasingly less time to socialize at leisure in the traditional offline environment. This phenomenon has driven the growth of online dating platforms, to help young people connect with prospective partners in a social networking environment.

India's social networking market has been spurred by demand for online dating and matchmaking sites like Shaadi.com. Some of China's largest social networks are essentially online dating platforms – with the promise of meeting people and going on dates – sometimes virtually – at the core of the offering. These dating communities enjoy loyal following and have great longevity in Asia.

Across Asian markets, the more entrenched versions of online dating platforms are consistently done well to nurture an early critical mass of followers, and to develop localized language and experiences that have provided a strong basis for sustaining loyal online communities, sometimes consisting of millions.

The local, entrenched, international, evolving experience

Asia has some of the earliest and most successful locally developed social networking sites, such as CyWorld, Mixi, Gree (Japan), Renren and QZone (China), establishing commandingly large and loyal user bases. These platforms have proved extremely successful and have thrived financially, with robust models that serve and monetize digital content, advertising and subscriptions.

Social networking in Asia keeps evolving though, as the major global players like Groupon, the social shopping site, and Facebook make massive investments across the region, with rich platforms and the promise of something new and exciting – as well as a larger online community to be part of.

There is no sure bet with social media and networking in Asia – sites that were popular as recently as a year ago in India, are now obsolete, and the same goes for China and other fast-developing large internet markets in Asia. I remember how, a year or so ago, a mobile microblogging platform called "SMS Gupshup" was doing extremely well in India and was getting a lot of press coverage. Within just a few months, the site had evaporated from the news feeds, and today I am not even sure if it still exists. In China, challenged by a heavy regulation of the internet, many social sites that are popular face the constant risk of being blocked and put out of business – relegated to an isolated patch on the dark side of the Great Firewall.

Asian internet users are still reluctant to pay for social network services – at least for entry. Once inside and loyal, with a community formed, users spend significant amounts on gaming and entertainment apps, as well as on virtual goods and currencies. In Asia, the virtual goods market has already grown into a multi-billion dollar industry – and it is as yet in its infancy.

Asia's biggest markets have been quick to embrace the international digital ecosystems of Yahoo! (very popular in Japan), Facebook (popular in every market other than in mainland China) and Twitter (again, everywhere but mainland China), adopting similar patterns as markets in Europe and North America.

Perhaps the only safe bet in terms of social networking platform adoption trends is that the list of accepted, popular sites will keep evolving and shifting. Unlike in the West, arguably, with the absolute dominance of Facebook today, in Asia's 35 markets there are no players that are so entrenched as not to be challenged or concerned about competition.

Time and time again we have seen the list of most popular platforms change, and there is no doubt, that over the next few years, we will witness more changes as newer social technologies emerge, and as new online consumption behaviour and habits take hold.

Diving deeper into Asian markets

While some areas, such as China and India, have internet penetration rates below 25 per cent others, like Hong Kong, South Korea, Japan, Australia and Singapore, boast numbers rivalling anywhere in the world.

Certain South East Asia markets, like Singapore, Indonesia and Malaysia have Facebook dominating the social networking space. In Vietnam, however – as in Mainland China – Facebook has been blocked by the government. As mentioned earlier, Indonesia is one of Twitter's biggest markets in terms of user penetration, and Jakarta, Indonesia's capital city, boasts 1 per cent of the world's tweets daily – giving it the dubious title of "the world's Twitter capital."

India, paradoxically, is one of Asia's largest social media markets in terms of sheer size and potential, but is one of the smallest in terms of internet penetration. India's potential has yet to be tapped – her growing, massive middle class of over 300 million people makes it a market to watch out for, as infrastructure develops and users connect with each other and brands and products online.

The South Korean social media market is one of Asia's most mature, and boasts internet usage penetration rates among the highest in the world. South Koreans love to comment and create positive content around brands and products – the perfect type of social media user. Blogging penetration is amazingly high in South Korea, with 92 per cent of the internet population there consuming blogs.

Asia, the future – charting a course ahead

So, the golden question in Asia remains: how can companies tap into the social media?

The year 2010 proved a milestone for digital penetration, communications, marketing and innovation in Asia. With rich media stories such as the continued ascendancy of social networking and media, the fevered speculation around Google's "exit" from China, the start of new social concepts such as location-based services [LBS] and group shopping the coming of age of social media as a mainstream channel for communications and marketing in Asia was writ as de-facto by the end of 2010.

Perhaps the most interesting trend was the phenomenal rise of microblogging in Asia, and in China, Sina's microblogging platform – Weibo, leading to spectacular issues, online crises, rumours, gossip and more dynamic ways for businesses to market and communicate.

Many companies in Asia still continue to struggle with the new realities of the real-time "social" web. Social technology advancements have fast and furiously altered the landscape of corporate reputation, brand management, public relations and market influence.

Recent studies of the space reveal how large organizations, and multinationals particularly, have yet to sustain cohesive strategies around digital engagement and social media. This is likely to change quickly over the next two years. If 2010 and 2011 represented a period of social media "experimentation" and "exploration" for institutions and companies in Asia, then 2012 and 2013 are surely the years of social media "commitment" – when individuals and businesses find their feet and make sense of social media in their lives, productively.

New forms of digital storytelling in Asia – data visualization

In Asia, infographics are often used to explain a myriad of topics, such as the rapid rise of the continent's national prosperity indices, to the region's diverse digital landscapes and online social communities.

Moving into the future, no business in Asia will be able to tell good stories to its stakeholders and consumers without visualizing ideas and data better. It is a concept that is being embraced by companies and by the PR, communications and marketing agencies that are charged with their stories.

This explains why infographics are increasingly being developed by Asian agencies and featured in communications and marketing campaigns, in both the online and offline arenas.

Roundup

Want more? See what has been said about this chapter or get involved and discuss it with the author and other readers on our LinkedIn group, find it by visiting http://www.socialmedia-mba.com or search for "The Social Media MBA Alumni".

Defining future trends is never an easy task. Nowhere is this more true than on the world's largest and most dynamic internet markets, with nearly a billion internet users already, and exponential growth upwards, more than anywhere else in the world, actively participating and spending more time in the social web.

The year 2012 promises to be even more interesting. Of course, Asia is a vast continent, far from homogenous, filled with a diversity of consumer behaviour and experience – from international metropolises like Shanghai and Mumbai, to tier two and three cities. But there are predications we can safely make, based on our understanding of Asia's fascinating digital communications landscapes.

Some safe predictions are that Asia is broadly the future, that no large company can afford not to be present here, and that no company in Asia can market and communicate successfully without developing a cohesive and sustainable social media strategy. And it must be a thoughtful strategy; one that speaks to its stakeholders in their own languages, in real time.

It truly is an exciting time to be living and working on social media in Asia, and as they say in China, "May you live in interesting times!"

In the next chapter Johan Bergelin will look beyond tactical tools to explore the common denominators for companies successful in social media.

Chapter 22

Why Lean and Six Sigma isn't enough anymore

Johan Bergelin

In short

- Why most executives are not fit to meet the challenges posed by social media.
- How creating experiences for consumers can open new doors.
- What the concept of design thinking can do for your social media strategy.

Overview

In this chapter Johan Bergelin based in Stockholm, currently Strategic Digital Director at Rewir and previously management consultant with Capgemini, will focus on the way leadership in organizations will need to change to meet the demands of a new kind of consumer that is armed not only with online technologies but also with a radically different mindset than generations before them.

In a digital world driven by social media, experiences will be your next differentiating edge and the efficiency driven leadership style of today will not be able to cope in creating those. To succeed you need a leadership style that celebrates creativity across your entire company, you need design thinking.

Johan Bergelin was once one of the most influential male fashion bloggers in Sweden, but has since then moved on to think strategically on the topics that made the blog so successful. Now he helps Swedish blue chip companies, primarily in the telecom and financial sectors, to succeed in an increasingly digital world designing branding strategies both for B2B and B2C companies.

I believe that the common denominator for successful companies in social media is ability to deliver a superior experience, experiences that are so rewarding for people that they have to, or actually desire to, share them with other people. It is really quite simple, we are back to the old town square where everyone knew where to get the best bread, the best meat or the best tools. As touched upon in Chapter 4, the reason that people knew this was not mass communicated advertising, it was rather good old fashioned word of mouth. The best businessman, as in the one providing the best goods, got the most customers because people shared their thoughts and opinions on the town square.

Today, the market place for those thoughts and opinions is not the town square; it is the internet, where millions of people participate in discussions that range from the trivial to insightful conversations around the most diverse topics. The hypothesis that I am arguing for is that this type of interactive communication will become more important for the purchasing decisions than traditional advertising. In the light of this reality, companies must realize that it is no longer what they say (as in advertising) that is the prime engine for building a strong brand and great customer relationships, it is what you do, as in the experience that you deliver, that drives social communication that can benefit you.

> In the light of this reality, companies must realize that it is no longer what they say (as in advertising) that is the prime engine for building a strong brand and great customer relationships, it is what you do.

To illustrate what I mean by delivering experiences as the most powerful form of communication, let's take a look at three different cases from significantly different industries.

Powerful experiences

Zappos, the online retailer that is famously known for extraordinary customer service, is maybe the best example that it *is* possible to build and run a billion dollar company that focuses on experiences rather than on advertising. Zappos started off selling shoes online but has now moved into offering a wide variety of products via their web site. However, their differentiation does not come from their product range, it comes from giving an unmatched customer service; they provide 24/7 phone customer service, they have 365 days return policy with free shipping in both directions and their personnel are famously known for truly delivering well over what you would expect from any company.

CEO Tony Hsieh calls this "delivering happiness", which is also the tagline for their whole company. He has moved the purpose of the company, the vision if you will, outside the company's own success. Their purpose is clear, they are here to deliver happiness and, frankly, they could really be selling anything under that vision. Of course, a vision like this entails more than just a catchy tagline, the company must in every part of its operations understand what it means to deliver happiness, from the call centre personnel to the accountant. Therefore, it is obvious that a social media strategy for a company like Zappos is in fact the same as their overall business strategy. They have built a company bottom up that is tailored to fit into a world that has gone social.

Saltå Kvarn is a producer of ecologically friendly produce in Sweden and is one of few brands that actually live up to and base their entire operations on a corporate social responsibility (CSR) agenda. They are trying to build a strong brand by essentially being a good company. Good in this case incorporates both the normal, old school good, which is running a healthy business, and good in the sense of doing good. In fact, their vision is maybe even more stunning than Zappos's. Saltå Kvarn's vision is to contribute to a healthier Baltic Sea. The Baltic Sea is today on its way to recovering from many years of pollution, both industrial pollution primarily from the southern countries surrounding it and, to a large extent, from fertilizers from Swedish farms. The experience they provide is a chance to save the Baltic Sea, one can of beans at a time.

Saltå Kvarn is heavily involved in social media, which for them has proven to be a very effective means of communication. Since they have such a strong vision that sits firmly outside their organization, they can easily utilize tactical opportunities when they appear. If, for example, there is a scandal in the way pigs are treated at farms they can easily respond to that event with comments or campaigns that are very much in line with their overall vision.

Moleskine is another great example of how a company uses experiences to drive conversation and brand building online. Moleskine, a company founded in 1997, produces notebooks. The mystery of the Moleskine success is fascinating: at the end of the day it is just a notebook that you use to scribble down ideas or notes from a meeting, something that you could easily do in any kind of notebook that would cost you substantially less than a Moleskine notebook.

But a Moleskine notebook is something else. The design comes from an old type of notebook that was used by intellectuals for a long time and when it went out of production in 1986 many writers and poets were disappointed. However, when Moleskine started production again in 1997 times were different. People started gathering online, creating communities and blogs around the notebook, sharing stories on how they used it and how they appreciated its robust design and classic look. It soon became a staple good for anyone that was an intellectual or just wanted to look like one. Moleskine understood the power in nourishing the myth that was created around the notebook. To use a Moleskine notebook should not feel like taking down notes on paper, to use a Moleskine product should feel like walking in the footsteps of Hemingway or Picasso.

Management strategy meets social media strategy

Creating experiences like these should be right in the middle of your social media strategy, simply because the real success in social media should and must be measured against how much activity you can create around your brand organically, not induced by social media campaigns and advertising. Such tools can be very good as complements and as tactical actions to strengthen the experience that you create; but if you can't back that story up with actions the interest will soon wane and discussions die out.

If experiences, created across the whole company, are the driving force to succeed in an interactive world it is not farfetched to claim that what used to be called a social media strategy actually is a strategy for the whole company. Looking at the examples above, one can conclude that their social media success has much more to do with their company strategy than it ever had to do with strategies that focus on which digital tools to use or who in the company should use them.

Another thing that these companies have in common is the way that they put the purpose of their company outside themselves. The actual reason for them to exist is in fact something larger than profit. For Zappos it is about "Delivering happiness", for Saltå Kvarn it is about saving the Baltic Sea and for Moleskine it is about creating an attachment with the history of intellectuals.

Management theoretician and consultant Simon Sinek has created a model that explains the benefit of doing this that he calls the "golden circle theory" (Sinek, 2009). The model is really simple, it consists of three words; why, how, what. The why is the reason for existing; the how is the processes and culture that you create; and the what is what you actually produce, whether it be services or products.

Most companies start from the outside (the what) going inwards (to the why) defining themselves with the products or services they produce. In this case the purpose, the why, becomes secondary instead of being the core of the company. A successful company, however, often starts with the why and lets products and service be of secondary nature. Zappos, for example, could essentially sell anything as long as it delivered happiness.

The golden circles model has been developed from insights on how our brains function when we make purchasing decisions. When making choices we first use the part of the brain used for emotions and feelings, only later do we use the part of the brain responsible for logic and rational behaviour. Hence, if we try to sell a product using only rational arguments, our brain does not respond well to this. Rationale and logic comes afterwards to prove to ourselves that we have made a good choice.

The why of an organization is the basis from which you should create the set of experiences that will best drive activity in social media. The experiences will, in turn, if they are amazing enough, create the necessary word of mouth and convey the message and values of the organization to everyone that tunes in to the discussion.

However, these are merely the goals that an organization should strive to achieve in order to be successful in an interactive world. There is nothing in what we have discussed so far that actually tells you how to achieve those goals. We have so far only sketched the future arena that companies need to act on, a new set of rules if you will. As in sports, a new set of rules usually change the way you play the game and in business life this translates into which kind of managerial approach you have.

The management style of the previous century was based more than anything on efficiency and quality. Management models such as Lean and Six Sigma were developed and implemented on such a scale that they have now impacted every sector and essentially every company. For consumers this is a good thing, we got cheaper products with higher quality. In fact, products nowadays are so good and so cheap, across the board, that those parameters less and less constitute a competitive advantage.

Efficiency and quality will still be cornerstones for profitable businesses in the future; the difference is that those parameters are becoming hygiene factors, not differentiating factors. If you don't deliver on the hygiene factors you are not even playing the game. To truly differentiate your company you need to deliver experiences to customers, real experiences that are emphatic, human and aesthetic, filled with emotions. Authenticity is key when you build a company for an interactive era when your customers will do the talking for you, since they will speak what they perceive as the truth, not your brand boiler plate.

To deliver outstanding experiences companies need to realize that experiences have to be innovated, just as products have been since the beginning of the industrial revolution. Great customer experiences do not come about by themselves: just as with any other innovation, to occur they need an environment where they can flourish and grow. However, innovation does not come naturally from an organization that focuses on efficiency. In Clayton M. Christensen's book, *The Innovators Dilemma* (1997), he shows with clarity that efficiency driven organizations usually are able to produce good pace of incremental innovation but rarely the big breakthroughs like capturing the benefits of a whole new technology.

Today you need a management style that emphasizes and rewards other kind of behaviours than efficiency; you need a management style that rewards creativity and exploration, that focuses on true human needs and desires. You need managers who are able to balance the logical and rational left hand side of the brain with the artistic and creative right hand side of the brain. In short, you need managers that are able to think like designers.

Design thinking to develop your social media strategy

Roger Martin, Dean of the Rotman School of Management in Toronto, is one of the academic forerunners of the management movement called design thinking. Design thinking, to sum it up briefly, is a school of thought where innovation and the creation of genuine experiences are placed right in the middle. Rogers argues, in his book *The Design of Business: Why Design Thinking is the Next Competitive Advantage* (2009), that traditional management styles have been focusing too much on inductive reasoning (observing that something works) and deductive reasoning (proving that something is) and too little on what he calls abductive reasoning (imagining what something could be). One of the best modern examples of this is something we are all familiar with and many of us probably hold quite dear, the iPhone. When Apple invented the iPhone they truly redefined what a phone could be and redefined a whole market.

Design thinking unlocks the possibilities for companies of all sorts to become masters of abductive thinking, to capture possibilities hidden for others and, most importantly of all in the context of this book, to create experiences that will grant you access to social media bliss. To describe what design thinking really is it is best to turn to one of the great masters and pioneers in the field, Tim Brown, CEO of design company IDEO, and his book *Change by Design: How Design Thinking Transforms Organizations and Inspires Innovation* (2009). IDEO's journey from a product design company to a company that creates complete brands and businesses is astonishing and they have done this by working with design thinking on a massive scale.

Design thinking is to apply the methodologies of a designer onto problems that do not involve designing an object but are rather problems that need to be solved. In essence what a designer does is to balance between what is *desirable* for humans, technologically *feasible* and what is *viable* from a business perspective to find remarkable solutions. All of these parameters need to be balanced in order to achieve great things (a beautiful product that is impossible to produce due to constraints in material or resources is, for example, useless, no matter how beautiful it is). This is radically different from many companies and organizations of today where innovation usually starts from a business perspective or a technological perspective.

Starting from a business perspective usually creates a creative squeeze since most companies of today are set up to be efficient. In an environment where efficiency is the only parameter by which innovations are measured, the innovations tend to be incremental and small (such as "how can we increase the mileage of last year's car for this year's model?").

Starting from a technological perspective, where the guys in R&D have come up with a great new technology there is a great risk that the product will have a hard time finding a place in the current business model and creating value. However, by balancing the three dimensions, like on a tightrope, and always keeping that human perspective in focus, great innovations and experiences can be created.

Design thinking also emphasizes what Tim Brown calls divergent and convergent thinking. Divergent thinking is very similar to Martin's abductive reasoning. Divergent thinking is about creating options to choose from, whereas convergent thinking is about removing options by making choices. Many corporations of today use an innovation model that is focused solely on the convergent part, where ideas and innovations are put through a rigorous process to see what could generate future revenue. This is all good and necessary but the problem is that most companies have no process of generating really groundbreaking ideas that move into the convergent phase. This is where the divergent thinking comes in. In design thinking the divergent phase aims to create an abundance of ideas, all balancing that fine line of *desirability, feasibility* and *viability*. You go about doing this by using a different set of methodologies than usually used in product development. You observe humans in the natural habitat, at home, at work and while travelling to see how they actually behave, not what they say in focus groups. Instead of sending out market research studies to get a clear picture of the "median person", you seek out extreme users in the category where you are trying to innovate (if you are in the toy industry, for example, you let kids roam your meeting rooms filled with toys and observe them). If you are looking to recreate the retail outlet experience of your brand, you don't ask customers how they would like it to be, you build cheap prototypes of the environment and act out role playing games where you, together with the customer, can get insights that further can refine your prototype into an actual retail design. It is all about gathering human focused insights of actual behaviours instead of using realms of data to create statistical averages of humans.

Prototyping is a key element of design thinking. Prototyping enables you to swiftly get a visual representation of what you are after that can be communicated to a broader audience within and outside your company and you should start to prototype early in the process. By creating a prototype you are forced to visually and physically show what you mean with an idea so that others can build on that idea and come up with ideas of their own. The prototypes do not have to be fancy and well designed; the important thing is to actually create them. If it doesn't work, so what, you did it very fast and cheap, let's do a new one. Fail early and finish sooner is a great thing to remember.

Prototyping is not only possible to use when it comes to physical objects, prototypes can be used just as well for abstract things like a service experience or an online web shop. With a little bit of imagination you can prototype essentially anything.

In *The Designful Company* (2008) Marty Neumeier describes a core difference between traditional modes of thinking and design thinking by looking at how MBA courses are usually taught, namely by case studies. The idea is that the best solution to a given business problem can be found by looking at a handful of companies that have successfully solved it and that that solution can be implemented across the board for all kinds of companies, something that management consultants often refer to as best practice.

Using a best practice approach, top management is often presented a set of readymade solutions that they can pick and choose from. This will probably solve the problem at hand but the model also assumes that no other solutions are available that actually could be better. Do you get what is right for you or just almost right? A better solution would be to design a number of solutions using the tools described so far in this chapter. That could be a difficult process but the reward is worth it since it gives you a chance to differentiate. This *modus operandi* creates a whole lot more insecurity than choosing from readymade solutions but that is in itself not wrong, it just creates a new kind of managerial challenge. As Jonathan Ivy, head designer at Apple says, "One of the hallmarks of the team is this sense of looking to be wrong . . . because then you know you've discovered something new" (Marty Neumeier, 2008).

Let's turn to a practical example where design thinking has proven to be extremely useful. This example is taken from *Change by Design: How Design Thinking Transforms Organizations and Inspires Innovation* (Brown, 2009).

Shimano applies design thinking

Do not look at this as a case (since we learnt that it could be detrimental for your innovative capabilities) but more as inspiration of the power of design thinking.

IDEO was approached by Japanese bike component manufacturer Shimano to help them design a new set of components. However, the brief was not as rigid as that, it was rather open ended and gave the design team opportunity to discover what could be done within the bike market. The team, consisting of anthropologists, engineers and designers (another trait of design thinking is that teams usually are cross functional) ventured into the field to perform the kind of studies described above. They observed, they talked to power bike users, they talked to people that never rode a bike and one of the main conclusions they came back with was that only 10 per cent of adult Americans rode a bike now while 90 per cent did ride a bike when they were younger. Somehow they stopped riding a bike as they were growing up. Inspired by this insight the team continued to dig deeper into the problem. One of the reasons was that it was a hassle to maintain complicated components and they were intimidated by the retail experience where more often than not they were met by a bike specialist dressed in spandex and with the body of an athlete. The bike market was essentially geared towards dedicated cyclists, not towards the massive 90 per cent casual biker market that did not ride a bike at all. This is what, in design thinking, would be called the *inspiration* stage. This is where you find the insights that you base your further work on.

The next stage is *ideation*. Ideation is essentially to work creatively with the insights to see how they can be converted into something tangible. In the Shimano case this eventually led to a solution where IDEO and Shimano not only constructed a new set of components but a whole bike concept, the Coaster bike. The concept included a reference design for a bike with no visible gears, no hand brakes but a back pedal brake and a clean relaxed feeling. However, the bike was not low tech, rather the opposite. To ensure a smooth ride the bike was equipped with an automatic gear system and high tech materials.

The concept did not stop there; as they moved into the *implementation* stage they also designed a retail store concept for the bike where you would be met not by cyclist athletes but by people like you and me in a non intimidating environment.

Shimano came to ask for a new set of components and in return they got a whole new biking concept where their components (the automatic gears) would be an integral part. Not only was it brilliant in that it expanded the current market for bikes from 10 per cent of the adult population, but it also made it very hard for other component manufacturers to copy their approach.

I have not even begun to cover every aspect of design thinking in this short chapter. It has more facets than are possible to describe and discuss in such a limited space that this chapter allows for. To get a full picture of what design thinking really is I recommend you read the books that are referenced in this chapter, and then dig even deeper if the topic interests you.

Roundup

Want more? See what has been said about this chapter or get involved and discuss it with the author and other readers on our LinkedIn group, find it by visiting http://www.socialmedia-mba.com or search for "The Social Media MBA Alumni".

Traditionally design has been brought into projects at the very end when it is time to put a nice plastic shell over an advanced piece of technology, but design has never really been a part of the whole creation process in most companies, neither at strategic level nor at tactical level.

As we move into the interactive, digital society this is bound to change. Consumers are fed up with settling for the generic, the mass produced goods of the industrial era and are looking for genuine and authentic experiences that they can feel an emotional attachment to. This is what will claim your space in the social media universe and the path that you need to take spells design thinking.

References

Christensen, C.M. (1997) *The Innovator's Dilemma: When New Technologies Cause Great Firms to Fall.* Harvard Business School Press.

Martin, R.L. (2009) *The Design of Business: Why Design Thinking is the Next Competitive Advantage.* Harvard Business School Press.

Neumeier, M. (2008) *The Designful Company: How to build a culture of nonstop innovation.* Peachpit Press.

Sinek, S. (2009) *Start with Why: How Great Leaders Inspire Everyone to Take Action.* Portfolio.

Chapter 23

Boris Veldhuijzen van Zanten

In short

- Why everyone will be famous for 15 people, not 15 minutes.
- How come some people argue that Google is God?
- What determines if a new social technology is here to stay and worth your time?

Overview

In this chapter serial internet entrepreneur Boris Veldhuijzen van Zanten discusses how the web, and technology, is making us more divine. How technology makes us more god-like and how we can judge what is "good" technology by comparing it to the kind of abilities a god would have.

There are five attributes to what makes a god a god. You would have to be omniscient (all-knowing), omnipresent (everywhere at once), omnibenevolent (always good), omnipotent (can do everything) and immortal (no physical presence). Technology and social media help us achieve those five things and, thus, make us more god-like.

You've come all the way to the last chapter in this book and no doubt you've gained a lot of knowledge and picked up some extremely useful tips. So now what? Where is the world of social media heading? How do you apply all that knowledge and what does it all lead to? How durable is this new phenomenon exactly and how much time and effort should we all invest in keeping up and taking advantage of it? These are tough questions to answer, but I'm planning on offering you a basic and simple formula to make sense of it all. Long story short: ask yourself if a technology makes you more divine.

I know, that last sentence begs for some explanation. Aspiring to be god-like and more divine can get you in trouble in a lot of places all around the world so it is not something to take lightly. It is, however, a very useful method to judge technology and innovation. When confronted with technology you should ask yourself; does it make me more divine? If the answer is yes, than by all means, invest time and effort. If the answer is no, it is time to move on.

To find out what divinity means it is important to define the word god. When you look at some of the more popular religions there are at least five attributes that define a god-like creature: gods are omniscient (all-knowing), omnipresent (everywhere at once), omnibenevolent (always good), omnipotent (can do everything) and immortal (no physical presence). It is my belief that modern technology is helping us attain all those qualities. Not perfectly and not as well as God Himself, but we are slowly getting there. Let me give you some examples of how different technologies help us become more divine, and how eventually you can use this to judge "good" from "bad" technology.

Omniscient

Humans have always strived to know more. We want to learn, know, find out the truth and always have access to all information about everything. This is of course what we think about when we picture an "all knowing" or "omniscient being". Although we know more now than we did before, we are still not close to knowing everything. But ever since Google became popular we have started to accept a different state of knowing. People accustomed to using Google feel like they know everything just because they can look up everything. I can answer almost any question you ask me, just by looking it up on

Google. We have started to accept Google as a natural extension of our brains. "I know the answer to that, I would just have to Google it first" is not a very unusual answer. It is also not very new. Older people often feel like they have an external extension of their brains: their partners. You know where the keys to the garage are because your partner knows, you know you are insured because your partner knows and you know who that person is that just waved at you as soon as your partner explains it to you. That is precisely the reason why older people who lose a partner often complain about feeling like they've lost half their brain. Half of their collective knowledge and memories are gone.

> We have started to accept Google as a natural extension of our brains. "I know the answer to that, I would just have to Google it first" is not a very unusual answer.

When I said earlier that Google could answer all my questions I was slightly exaggerating of course. There is a lot of information that can't be found on Google. However, that doesn't stop a group of people from asking "is Google God?" Calling themselves "The Church of Google" (http://www.thechurchofgoogle.org), they have published a list of nine proofs that Google is in fact God. And these aren't just theories either. According to their website these are "scientifically verified" facts. The group claims that Google is better at answering prayers, is omnipresent and accessible through mobile devices and from anywhere in the world. Proof number eight is my favourite: according to Google trends, the term "Google" is searched for more than the terms "God", "Jesus", "Allah", "Buddha", "Christianity", "Islam", "Buddhism" and "Judaism" combined. Google might not be more knowledgeable than God but she certainly is more popular.

Technology offers us easier, and more available, access to knowledge. In effect that makes us more omniscient and, thus, more divine.

Omnipresent

What is the most uttered sentence on mobile phones? It must surely be "where are you?" Location apparently gives a lot of context. It tells us whether you will listen patiently (at home, doing nothing), will be distracted (on my way home in the car) or whether you will have to keep it short (at the cash register in the supermarket). Entrepreneurs have jumped on this opportunity with location based social (LBS) networks and things like Facebook Places. Technology makes location both more prevalent and less important. With smart phones, lighter laptops and mobile phones location basically becomes irrelevant. I didn't use an old fashioned and heavy mechanical typewriter to write these words but my iPhone, iPad and laptop, and I used them in a local swimming pool while my kids were swimming, on the rooftop of our office building and at home in bed. These technologies make the idea of time, space and distance irrelevant. My documents are hosted in "the cloud", accessible with a wide variety of devices, at any moment and from any location. We are both hyper-present (our location is shared and known) and hypo-present. It really doesn't matter where we are, but we will measure our location every second and share it with whoever wants to know it.

Omnibenevolent

Yes, technology stimulates you to be good. Google will archive every indexable deed you perform whether it is good or bad. eBay will keep track of how you treat your customers and adjust your rank accordingly, and your former co-workers will haunt you on LinkedIn and Facebook forever. Screw one over and you will never get rid of them. Being a crook is hard, on the internet. The tools to do wrong are easy to find and readily available. Unfortunately the internet's memory is stronger than an elephant's and less forgiving.

In 1996 I accessed the web for the first time. My father bought a modem, we spent hours getting it to work and browsed the web for the first time seated behind his Mac. It was magical. After a few hours he left me alone with the computer and went to bed. So what does a teenager with access to the web do when he gets alone? He searches for sex, naturally. I made sure I was alone, browsed to Altavista (the dominating search engine at that time) and entered my search query: sex. Nervously I clicked the first result. Of course, there was no sex on the first search result but a form welcoming me to the

"Searches for Sex" experiment page of a certain college professor with a sense of humour. He had set up this page to find out how many people were searching for "Sex" on the web by counting the number of visitors to his page. Slightly disappointed but also amused I decided to leave a comment. There were three other people who commented too, I left the fourth comment.

Up until 2004, whenever you typed my name into Google, the first result was always "Boris Veldhuijzen van Zanten searched for Sex on the Web" with a link to that page where thousands of comments had been left ever since.

Some people see this as a loss of privacy and something to regret. Personally I don't. Sure, the example above was slightly embarrassing, until you realize that most young people have done the same thing. Posting your drunk photos to Facebook is considered a bad idea by some people. After all, your future employer might see them and think less of you – unless of course everybody posts their silly photos to Facebook. If you were the only one not doing it your employer might suspect even worse from you. And believe me, even your employer did things he or she regretted later. So is privacy over? No, it is just changing. Andy Warhol once said that "In the future, everyone will be famous for 15 minutes". That future has come and gone. Right now everyone is famous for 15 people. You might have some followers on Twitter, maybe even more than 15, but that is about the audience you are dealing with. The updated wisdom about privacy used to be that "In the future, everyone will be anonymous for 15 minutes". But with 5 per cent of all babies under two having a social media profile and when you realize that 23 per cent (http://thenextweb.com/socialmedia/2010/10/06/5-of-unborn-babies-have-a-social-media-profile/) of all foetuses have images of their antenatal scans uploaded before birth, you realize that even those 15 minutes of privacy are too much to ask.

> Andy Warhol once said that "In the future, everyone will be famous for 15 minutes". That future has come and gone. Right now everyone is famous for 15 people.

New technology makes it attractive for us to sacrifice our privacy but as a side effect it also stimulates us, often strenuously, to become more honest and less deceiving.

Omnipotent

There is no doubt in my mind that technology makes us more powerful and I don't think many people will argue against this notion. We can reach people all around the world, and with minimal effort, day and night, from the comfort of our sofas, beds or bathrooms. Digital cameras allow us to take photos at minimal cost and multiply and share them with anyone. Compare that to the days where you arrived home from school to find the vacation shots had arrived back from the developer. Usually this took a few weeks and you would have 30 or 40 photos to go through. Now, we use our mobile phones to share those photos via Twitter and Facebook with our families and friends within seconds of taking them. When you buy an Apple computer it comes preloaded with an application called Garageband. It gives you access to almost every known instrument and recording tool that were once only affordable for rich musicians. Having access to those tools doesn't mean you automatically become as talented as The Beatles, but just imagine how many young people, with talent, suddenly are empowered with access to tools that were once only available to a small elite. Then once they master these tools, and produce their masterpieces, their audiences are only a click away. Numerous musicians have been discovered, literally overnight, by uploading their home recorded songs and video clips to YouTube. The examples of technology empowering humans are numerous and we experience them every day. Technology clearly helps us become more powerful and potent.

Immortal

Unfortunately we haven't found the elixir that gives us eternal life. If we had, I would have surely read about it on Twitter. What we can do, however, is record our memories, indefinitely. Although we might grow old and die, our lives are well recorded and stored online for everybody to experience and explore. Surely that makes us slightly less mortal? And even if we really want to live forever there is hope. Some scientists are confident that the problem of death will be solved within the next 20 to 30 years. And even if you die there is a special social network just for you. Respectance.com is a social network for the deceased. That is a pretty ingenious proposition from the founders of that service. After all, none of their members will ever leave. Talk about customer loyalty there.

The idea behind Respectance.com is that once you pass away your loved ones will use your profile as a permanent online memorial dedicated to your life. Your friends and family will be able to add stories about you, including photos and videos, and leave public comments and talk to other people who miss you. You might be gone physically but you will live on forever in the memories of your friends and in the digital archives, spread out over dozens of servers, on the web.

Technology

As you can see, technology is a great enabler. It helps you become more powerful, knowledgeable, honest, present and it will even make you immortal, in a way. Technology makes you more divine and more god-like. You might argue that this is blasphemous but I'm not too worried about that. Wanting to be as good as a god can only be considered a compliment. As the saying goes, "imitation is the greatest form of flattery".

From God to social media

A few weeks ago I had the chance to sit down with the CEO of a mobile operator. This is a multi-billion dollar company with over 1,000 employees, a lot of customers and international influence. I was introduced as an "internet guy" so the first question the CEO asked me was "so what do you think about the crazy valuation of Facebook?" As I pondered the question he answered it himself "I don't see how they are ever going to make money".

This wasn't a dumb person. In fact, this was probably one of the smartest guys I've ever met. Still, his remark was very disappointing to me. Disappointing because it lacked creativity or even the will to think beyond the obvious. I couldn't resist and told him "you are a pretty smart guy. Are you going to tell me that if I put you in charge of 500 million loyal customers you wouldn't know how to make money off of them?"

The challenge for Facebook, or Twitter or any other company with a lot of users, isn't whether they can make money. They all can. In fact, Facebook did a rumoured 800 million in revenue in 2009 and announced they broke even. This year, the company will reportedly cross the 1 billion mark. Generating money is not the problem when you are the number one website in the world, as Facebook currently is.

The real challenge is relevance

How do you stay relevant with 500 million or 1 billion members? How do you make sure you don't turn into the next ICQ, Orkut or Myspace? Finding the answer to relevance is a lot harder than answering the "money" question. And I can guarantee that this is what keeps people at those companies awake at night. Is that unreasonable? Do you think that nothing can destroy the growth of Facebook?

Unfortunately history has proven that people are extremely fashion cautious, disloyal and eager to move on to the next best thing. I remember when Friendster grew to 10 million members overnight and friends of mine announced they were starting their own social network: "suckers!" is what I thought. I reasoned that with 10 million members nobody would ever catch up to Friendster. They had what investors call, and love, the "first mover advantage". Well, we all remember what happened to Friendster (my friends turned their social network into a thriving and very profitable business and the only local network that beats Facebook in their market).

Then history repeated itself with MySpace; untouchable, growing exponentially and eventually backed by Newscorp they seemed like the next, well, Facebook.

And now we are all stuck at Facebook. Us, our friends, our family and every old friend you hoped to forget and never see again. Is Facebook unstoppable? Of course not.

Let's imagine that in a month or so a new network arises. Maybe it will be started by two guys in a garage, or by Google, or by Apple. It really doesn't matter who will start it. What matters is that it will be cooler than Facebook. You won't find out about it until the three people around you who are cooler than you start inviting you. You will check it out, not understand the interface at first, but you will see that something cool is going on. Also, your mother won't be there: just the cool people.

So you cautiously switch. After a week or two you find out that you are spending more and more time on the new thing. So you invite your friends. Heck, you connect to Facebook and Gmail and invite ALL your contacts. Within a month or two they all switch over too.

Sure, the children will stay behind, and so will the elders. But the cool majority will have no problem with switching to where the cool kids hang out. It doesn't matter how cool that bar is where everybody hangs out: if your friends move to the new hot bar next door, you will follow.

Roundup

Want more? See what has been said about this chapter or get involved and discuss it with the author and other readers on our LinkedIn group, find it by visiting http://www.socialmedia-mba.com or search for "The Social Media MBA Alumni".

What happens if the social tide turns? Suddenly all that revenue, all those status updates and all those connections are worthless. Facebook will have lost its relevance in an ever changing world and will never get it back.

Will that happen? It might not. But the chances of it happening are a lot higher than Facebook not finding a way to make money. And where there is money there is opportunity to innovate.

CONCLUSION

Christer Holloman

As you might recall from my introduction I set out to create the book that I wish had been available when I was in your position. A book for people that work with social media on a daily basis, within organizations that adopted social media a long time ago, but that felt there is an opportunity to do it more or do it better and needed some serious inspiration and advice.

Over the past pages we have read the thoughts of and results created by some of the most progressive social media practitioners around. I hope reading this book has been as rewarding for you as developing it was for me. Every new page submitted by a contributor was like opening Christmas presents that I unwrapped as quickly as I could. While reading I was continuously asking myself: how could I apply this to my own social media work, how does this relate to my employer, my client and my own understanding of the potential business application of social media?

Among what we have learnt there are some key points that really speak to me namely:

- The need to continuously question my social media strategy, as we accumulate more learnings, as new social media channels come and as our competitors get more sophisticated with their social media.
- Always assign an ROI target for each social media endeavour, don't be afraid to hold it accountable for our time.
- Social media can't be the responsibility of the marketing department alone if we want to make it scalable and win us new business.

In fact I think this last point is the biggest game changer that we are facing, to get your organization to accept that social media isn't a marketing tool but something that should be as integrated and natural as the air a company breathes. I appreciate this sounds a bit fluffy, so the challenge is to get the message across in such a way that you can secure buy-in from the leadership team. How can the different departments around you leverage social media to achieve their objectives?

I've found that the most efficient way to spread the adoption of social media internally is by doing before asking. Depending on the type of company you work for, is there an opportunity for you to use your digital assets in a new way via social channels? Can you host a workshop with some key people from different departments to review what others are doing to get your own creative juices flowing? What if you had to set up your company today from scratch and built it on Facebook, what would it look like?

One thing is for sure, the more noise you make about this, increasingly your colleagues will turn to you for guidance and advice, embrace that opportunity to confirm your position. Make sure you can give good answers by keeping up to date with the latest developments and connect with peers via networking events in your area or online, share your insight and listen in to their conversations.

One quick and easy step is to join our Alumni group, find it by visiting http://www.socialmedia-mba.com or search for "The Social Media MBA Alumni" on LinkedIn. It's a forum where you can share your own case studies, exchange ideas, ask questions or perhaps look around for new job openings or recruit people with a social media track record to your own team.

With that said, I think it is time to thank you for your attention and wish you all the best with making a difference where you are.

Class dismissed!

BIOGRAPHIES

Eb Adeyeri

LONDON – SENIOR DIGITAL STRATEGIST AT 360° DIGITAL INFLUENCE, OGILVY PUBLIC RELATIONS WORLDWIDE (www.ogilvypr.com)

Eb is a digital strategist at Ogilvy's 360° Digital Influence team. Prior to this, he headed up the digital team for the UK office of LEWIS PR. Eb was a very early adopter of social media and pretty much has a profile on every social network around. He provides strategic advice on how to implement digital tactics within marketing and PR campaigns, manage online communities as well as the tools to measure and track success. In addition to this, he is instrumental in providing creative ideas that underpin many of these campaigns.

Eb has worked with the likes of Salesforce, Autoglass and Pret A Manger in developing and project managing socially led campaigns that have not only helped these brands raise the levels of engagement with their stakeholders but also helped improve their bottom lines. In 2011, Eb was named as one of PRWeek's Power Players of Social Media.

Email: eb.adeyeri@gmail.com   LinkedIn: uk.linkedin.com/in/eadeyeri
Twitter: @eba   Blog: ebtwopointzero.net/

Johan Bergelin

STOCKHOLM – STRATEGIC DIRECTOR DIGITAL AT REWIR (www.rewir.se)

Currently Johan is Strategic Director Digital at the branding agency Rewir. He has been running their digital practice since the spring of 2010 with a focus on making sure that their clients' brands live and breathe on the web in the same manner as they do offline.

Johan lives and breathes the web 24 hours a day and has done so since he first started using a modem and browsed BBS forums. Much has happened since then but a passion for the digital life remains and is as strong as ever.

In his work with digital media he blends the insights he gained as management consultant at Capgemini Consulting for six years with the tools and behaviours of the online community world.

He was once one of the most influential male fashion bloggers in Sweden but has since then moved on to think strategically on the topics that made the blog so successful. Now Johan helps Swedish blue chip companies primarily in the telecom and financial sectors to succeed in an increasingly digital world designing branding strategies both for B2B and B2C companies.

Email: johan.bergelin@gmail.com   LinkedIn: se.linkedin.com/in/johanbergelin

Twitter: @johanbergelin   Website/Blog: www.averycommonview.com/

Ged Carroll

Hong Kong and London – Director Digital Strategies, Ruder Finn (www.rfistudios.com)

Ged has 14 years consumer and media marketing experience. He has developed successful brand marketing campaigns across Europe, East Asia and North America. His brand experience includes Motorola, Novartis, Malaria Consortium, The UN, Yahoo! and Sony.

Ged is a member of the CIPR (Chartered Institute of Public Relations), and was a guest lecturer on interactive marketing at LaSalle Business and Engineering School, Universitat Ramon Llull in Barcelona.

Email: gcarroll@ruderfinn.co.uk, renaissancechambara@mac.com
Twitter: @r_c

LinkedIn: uk.linkedin.com/in/gedcarroll
Blog: renaissancechambara.jp/

Jed Hallam

London – Communities Director at VCCP (www.vccp.com/)

Jed works at VCCP Share, the part of the VCCP Partnership that focuses on helping brands to connect with their stakeholders more effectively using social media and technology. Amongst others, he currently works with O2, MoreTh>n, News International and McDonald's.

A large part of what motivates Jed is how social networks and media are changing the way in which people build brands. He believes that we've never been so connected and understanding how social media effects every part of a business will help us to plug the brand gap that exists for many businesses around the world.

Before working at VCCP, Jed spent three years as head of innovation and strategy Wolfstar, a consultancy that specialized in social media. While there, he worked with Discovery Channel, Sony Ericsson, GlaxoSmithKline, Unilever and first direct. He is also one of AdAge's top 150 marketing bloggers, he was listed as one of PRWeek's 29 under 29 in 2010 and has had his work published and featured in various national and international newspapers.

Email: jedh@vccp.com

LinkedIn: uk.linkedin.com/in/jedhallam

Twitter: @jedhallam

Blog: jedhallam.com/

Tim Hoang

LONDON – SENIOR SOCIAL MEDIA CONSULTANT AT VIVAKI (www.vivaki.com/)

Tim Hoang is the Senior Social Media Consultant at VivaKi and has worked on developing the social media strategies for a variety of clients. From B2B manufacturing technology to pet insurance companies, Tim has implemented campaigns across a range of industries.

His previous work includes helping brands such as Intel, Gillette and Colgate integrate digital channels into their existing communications strategies and establishing, building and managing communities for the likes of Acas (the Advisory, Conciliation and Arbitration Service), Ebico and John Lewis. He also created and ran social media training days for international clients such as ExxonMobil and Bank of America, and organized blogger events for Ferrero.

Tim was recognized by PRWeek as one of the top 29 PR professionals under the age of 29 for his digital expertise and reputation in the industry. He was also one of the co-founders of Twestival – the Twitter-based meet up which has raised over $1 million for charities in Africa.

Email: timhoang1982@gmail.com

LinkedIn: uk.linkedin.com/in/timhoang1982

Twitter: @timhoang

Blog: timhoang.wordpress.com/

Neville Hobson

LONDON – CONSULTANT (www.nevillehobson.com/)

Neville Hobson is an IABC-accredited communicator, blogger and podcaster, a writer and frequent speaker on digital media trends that matter to organizations.

He is an entrepreneur, early adopter (and leaver) and experimenter with digital technologies including social media, risk-assessing their impacts, roles and potential in organizational communication. He has more than 25 years' experience in public and media relations, marketing communication, employee, compensation and benefits communication as well as investor and financial relations.

Neville is a founding Senior Research Fellow and Advisory Board member of the Society for New Communications Research, a California-based non-profit think tank. He co-presents the weekly "For Immediate Release: The Hobson & Holtz Report" business podcast started in 2005.

Email: neville.hobson@gmail.com   Website/Blog: www.nevillehobson.com/
Twitter: @jangles   Podcast: www.forimmediaterelease.biz/
LinkedIn: www.linkedin.com/in/neville

David Marrinan-Hayes

LONDON – COMMERCIAL DIRECTOR AT ARCHANT
(www.archant.co.uk/)

Prior to his current role David was the head of product for Trinity Mirror Plc, the UK's largest newspaper group, where he was responsible for all digital product development and management.

He has worked for a variety of media organizations and startups in product development, digital editorial and strategy roles including BBC Worldwide, Conde Nast and Review Centre.

David is also currently director of collaborative consumption startup Lets-AllShare.com a peer-to-peer renting and lending site.

Email: dhayes22@mac.com   LinkedIn: uk.linkedin.com/in/davidmarrinanhayes

Twitter: @dmarrinanhayes   Blog: davidmarrinanhayes.tumblr.com/

Michael Netzley PhD

SINGAPORE – ASSISTANT PROFESSOR AT SINGAPORE MANAGEMENT UNIVERSITY
(www.smu.edu.sg)

Michael teaches corporate reputation and digital media at Singapore Management University. He has led numerous executive leadership programmes around the globe and has also held visiting professorships in Finland, Slovenia and Japan. In 2010 he was a research fellow with the Society for New Communication Research.

Michael is active as both a researcher and weekly correspondent to the *For Immediate Release* podcast.

Email: communicateasia@gmail.com   LinkedIn: sg.linkedin.com/in/michaelnetzley

Twitter: @communicateasia   Blog: communicateasia.asia

Zaheer Nooruddin

HONG KONG – DIGITAL CHIEF MARKETING OFFICER AT BURSON-MARSTELLER ASIA-PACIFIC (www.burson-marsteller.com)

Zaheer is the Digital Chief Marketing Officer for the Asia-Pacific region at global PR and communications firm Burston-Marsteller. He is also the firm's Lead Digital Strategist for Greater China and Practice Head of D/BM, Burson-Marsteller China's integrated digital and social media influencer practice.

During his 14-year career in integrated marketing communications around the world, Zaheer has worked in senior roles at international digital agencies, including Proximity Worldwide, Wunderman, Ogilvy and Edelman Digital.

A thought-leader on Online Social Communities and Networks in China and Asia, Zaheer speaks regularly at digital conferences and forums. He leads workshops on digital and social media strategy for B2B and B2C businesses in Asia.

A global citizen, Zaheer was born in India, spends his leisure time in Japan, and works in China and Asia. He is currently based in Hong Kong.

Email: zaheer.nooruddin@bm.com

Twitter: @zooruddin

LinkedIn: hk.linkedin.com/in/zaheernooruddin

Blogs and Life-streams:

bmdigitalchina.com/,

zaheernooruddin.info/

Euan Semple

LONDON – CONSULTANT (www.euansemple.com)

Euan Semple is one of the few people in the world who can turn the complex world of social networking into something we can all understand. And, at the same time, learn how to get the most from it. Ten years ago, while working in a senior position at the BBC, Euan was one of the first to introduce what have since become known as social media tools into a large, successful organization. He has subsequently had five years of unparalleled experience working with organizations such as Nokia, The World Bank and NATO. He is a one-man digital upgrade option for us all to download. The world is changing fast, but he makes sense of it because he understands that the core basics remain the same: community, learning, interaction. He is a master story-teller who offers a host of practical tales about how this new world can work for real people in the real world.

Email: euan@euansemple.com   LinkedIn: uk.linkedin.com/in/euansemple

Twitter: @euan   Blog: euansemple.com/theobvious/

Max Tatton-Brown

LONDON – ACCOUNT MANAGER AT EML WILDFIRE
(www.emlwildfire.com/)

Max is one of a generation of marketers who started their career just as social networks were beginning to exert influence on the industry. Previously at global agency AxiCom and now top ten UK tech agency EML Wildfire, he understands the value of integrated and sustainable marketing because, frankly, he's never practiced any other way of doing things.

Having managed worldwide campaigns for growing tech brands, Max's experience primarily involves innovative B2B businesses whose creations are designed to shake up the enterprise and establish future standards. From open source to virtualization to digital marketing and customer experience, there's a good chance you're using one of them in your business right now.

He blogs on industry and tech thoughts at MaxTB.com as well as contributing to other publications and collaborative projects.

Email: maxtattonbrown+book@gmail.com   LinkedIn: uk.linkedin.com/in/

Twitter: @maxtb   maxtattonbrown

www.google.com/profiles/maxtattonbrown   Blog: www.maxtb.com

Boris Veldhuijzen van Zanten

AMSTERDAM – SERIAL INTERNET ENTREPRENEUR, BLOGGER AND SPEAKER (www.thenextweb.com)

Boris started his first company V3 Redirect Services in 1997 and sold it in 1999 to Fortunecity.com. Thereafter, he started a Wi-Fi Hotspot operator in the Netherlands and sold to KPN after two years.

Since then he has started several projects and companies including The Next Web Conference and more recently TwitterCounter.com which is a premium analytics service for Twitter.

Email: bomega@me.com   LinkedIn: nl.linkedin.com/in/borisvvz

Twitter: @boris   Blog: thenextweb.com/, bomega.com

Jeremy Woolf

HONG KONG – SENIOR VICE PRESIDENT, GLOBAL SOCIAL MEDIA AND DIGITAL PRACTICE LEAD AT TEXT 100 (www.text100.com/)

Jeremy Woolf has worked in PR and marketing in Asia Pacific for more than 18 years, with expertise in a wide range of communications disciplines.

He oversees Text 100's global Social Media and Digital Practice, directing a global team responsible for product and service creation, creative client consulting and supporting staff digital skills development.

Woolf has managed programmes for blue chip and mid-sized clients worldwide including NXP, KEF and Alibaba.com. He is a frequent contributor to industry publications and an in-demand public speaker.

Email: woolf.jeremy@gmail.com　　LinkedIn: hk.linkedin.com/in/jeremywoolf

Twitter: @jeremywoolf　　Blog: publicrelationships.blogspot.com/

Alex Yenni

NEW YORK – SENIOR STRATEGIST FOR GLOBAL MULTIDISCIPLINARY AGENCY SAPIENTNITRO (www.sapient.com/)

Alex is a digitally focused brand strategist with nearly a decade of experience representing brands between San Francisco, London and New York. He has worked with clients large and small to create bespoke digital campaigns, including the likes of MediaCom, where he acted as the North American social media lead for the Glaxo-SmithKline's consumer product group (everything from Aquafresh to Tums), and Vonage, where he most recently served as Director of Social Media. He takes an integrated, multi-disciplinary approach to digital distribution, incorporating organic, paid media and production-based efforts. He currently serves as a senior strategist for global IT leader SapientNitro and is a principal consultant for branded content production house Invisible North.

Email: ayenni@gmail.com   LinkedIn: www.linkedin.com/pub/alex-yenni/2/b22/23b
Twitter: @1alex1   Blog: alexyenni.com

Simon Young

*AUCKLAND – PARTNER AND CONNECTOR AT SY-ENGAGE
(www.sy-engage.com/)*

Simon is Partner and Connector at sy-ENGAGE, a consultancy firm that specializes in creating possibilities through social engagement. sy-ENGAGE has worked with global brands such as Fonterra and Air New Zealand to create engagement leading to business results, both internally and externally. Simon has been a thought leader in the online communications space since 2001, having written many articles on the future of marketing, management and innovation. Simon's also a sought-after public speaker, having spoken and presented in China, Australia and New Zealand, including presenting courses for the University of Auckland and guest lecturing at the University of Otago.

Email: simon@sy-engage.com   LinkedIn: nz.linkedin.com/in/simonnyoung
Twitter: @simonyoung   Blog: simonyoung.co.nz/

INDEX

Index compiled by Liz Granger